Our
Souls

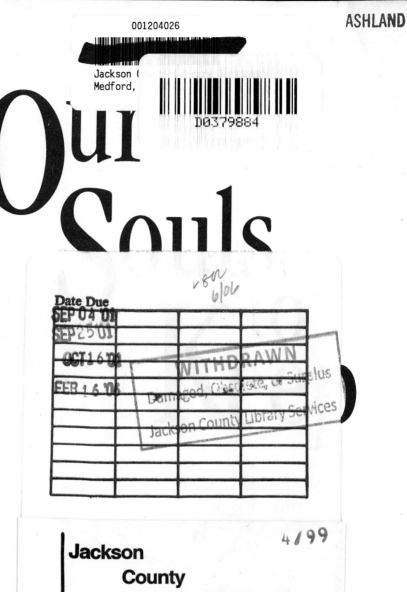

Our Souls to Keep

Black/White
Relations in America

George Henderson

Intercultural Press, Inc.
P.O. Box 700
Yarmouth, ME 04096 USA
207-846-5168

© 1999 by George Henderson

Book design and production by Patty J. Topel
Cover design by Patty J. Topel

Printed in the United States of America

03 02 01 00 99   1 2 3 4 5

Library of Congress Cataloging-in-Publication Data
Henderson, George, 1932–
    Our souls to keep: Black/white relations in America/
George Henderson.
        p. cm.
    Includes bibliographical references (p.   ) and index.
    ISBN 1-877864-65-X
    1. United States—Race relations. 2. African Ameri-
cans—History.   3. African Americans—Social conditions—1975–   4. African American children—Education. I. Title.
E185.615.H363   1998
305.896'073.—dc21   98–29811
                                                     CIP

To Louis and Jordan, my next generations of hope

Contents

Part III.   Conclusion

Preface

Two decades and many heartaches ago, one of my daughters came home from school in tears. "I'm not going back...the kids are horrible. They call me 'nigger.' Why don't they like me, Daddy?"

She was one of a handful of black children attending the predominantly white school. I gave her a long rambling answer, most of it forgotten by the next day. But we both still remember my concluding words: "They don't dislike you. They don't know you. They dislike what they think you are: an inferior person."

Since that time, I have been on a mission to help as many white people as I can to learn more about black Americans. Not just about the caricatures of blacks portrayed in movies and television shows or super-duper athletes but also about the other blacks, people who are mirror images of whites. My quest has taken me to countless private and public activities. But I only give bits and pieces of the story. In 1995 David Hoopes, editor-in-chief of Intercultural Press, asked me to put my perceptions and writings into a single, cohesive book. That set in motion a journey that had numerous twists and turns. At first, my rage spilled out incoherently onto the pages. Patiently, gently, and firmly David challenged me to set aside my negative feelings, or at least recast them into constructive prose, in order to produce a book that would be helpful to whites interested in rapprochement with blacks.

Then came Judy Carl-Hendrick, managing editor of Intercultural Press. She was given the task of shepherding the project to completion. Conferring with David, Toby Frank, president of Intercultural Press, and Karen Hall, editorial coordinator, Judy engaged me intellectually and emotionally. She pointed out reckless rhetoric, praised passages that were illuminating, and suggested ways to rewrite and reorganize portions of the manuscript. Indeed, her editing was a labor of love. Her comments were resolutely surgical. It was a tremendous black-white encounter that enriched all of us. Thus Judy, David, Toby, and Karen helped me to clearly focus *Our Souls to Keep*. I thank them for the good portions of the book, and I accept full responsibility for the aspects that fall short of the mark.

Like most of my daughter's classmates who got to know her, and became friends with her, I hope that whites who read this book will get to know more about blacks, and like some of us because of it. In any case, this book is my attempt to cross the racial divide that separates most blacks and whites.

—George Henderson

Copyright
Acknowledgments

Introduction: Behaviors that Separate Us

By dedicating themselves to living an Old Testament message (later inscribed on the Liberty Bell)—"Proclaim liberty throughout all the land unto all the inhabitants thereof"—the colonists of what is now the eastern United States made a landmark decision in human relations. Americans became the first people in history to commit themselves to the principles of democracy as a nation. Although tried on a small scale in several other countries of the world, only America dared to adopt nationally the axiom that "all men are created equal." Even then, however, the not-too-silent majority within the colonies was already behaving as though some people were more equal than others. Thus, from the birth of our nation, the pattern of inequality, prejudice, and racism was set.

During World War I, Vicente Blasco Ibáñez (1919) wrote *The Four Horsemen of the Apocalypse*, taking the title from the four horsemen described in the last book of the Bible, Revelation, which is also called the Apocalypse. He identified war, famine, pestilence, and death as the eternal curses of humankind. More recently, other writers identified four different horsemen: power, pollution, population, and prejudice—and this last horseman, prejudice, is the greatest obstacle to black Americans living full lives and sharing equally the abundant riches of the nation.

We all make negative decisions about people and ideas. However, being against someone or something is not necessarily a prejudice. For example, a white person is not behaving prejudicially if concluding after interacting with blacks that he or she doesn't like *those particular* black persons. But few people collect enough facts to allow them to make objective racial judgments. True prejudices are those negative attitudes directed toward groups, especially racial and religious groups, that are formed by highly personal and unreasoned generalizations about all or most members of the group ("You know how *those* people are!"). Prejudice results in the formation of ingroups and outgroups. We are employed, housed, married, and buried with one major criterion in mind: our group affiliations. The behaviors, customs, and speech of outgroup people are labeled "strange" and "inferior." Whites learn to dislike blacks, blacks learn to dislike whites, and other ethnic minority groups learn to dislike both blacks and whites—and each other.

Ignorance is one of the primary causes of prejudice. Without knowing the values and beliefs of other people, we cannot fully appreciate their goals and expectations and the rationale for their behavior, their cultural backgrounds and the contributions they have made or are able to make to society. Nor do we know what they have in common with us. Indifference is at one end of the continuum of ignorance; hostility is at the other.

But ignorance is not the only cause of racial prejudice. Colleges and universities have their share of well-educated but extremely racially prejudiced faculty, staff, and students. Their prejudices are deeply rooted in emotions that persist even when these intellectuals know that scientific studies have concluded that racial prejudice is based not on facts but on fear and that fear is based on insecurity. Many white professors who are prejudiced against blacks are fearful that if blacks ever reach positions of power, they will imitate racist whites and become hostile and repressive. Thus, *insecurity* is a second cause of prejudice. The irrational hatred among intellectuals makes it evident that although scientific studies are necessary, they are not enough to prevent prejudices from forming.

Group prejudices are expressed in terms of *stereotypes*— overgeneralized and often false images of outgroups: "Jews are pushy," "Blacks are lazy," "Japs are sneaky," "Poor whites are dumb." Clearly these group images are largely false, but they trigger the premature social and psychological deaths of the individuals so labeled. In most instances, these images can be destroyed only after the prejudiced person has had a positive experience with one or more members of the stereotyped group. But even this is often not enough. It is possible that a positive experience will only cause the prejudiced person to make an exception for that one individual by saying, "That person is different, exceptional, not like the others of the group."

Daily we witness the negative effects of racial prejudice. It creates inequalities, exclusions, and an atmosphere of rejection which prevent some groups of people from being allowed into mainstream American life. Prejudice is like a terrible cancer, engulfing the entire body, mind, and spirit, often defying the skills of those who wish to intervene.

Being a black person in the United States means living with the great probability of experiencing the outcomes of racial prejudice: personal insults from whites; poorer quality care or service than whites receive from physicians, criminal justice officials, teachers and school administrators, and other professionals; employment and housing discrimination; and threats, intimidation, and violence. Not every black person experiences all of these, but each has experienced some of them.

Certainly, all of the plight of blacks cannot be directly attributed to white prejudice and hatred. Some of it comes from shortsighted government programs and regulations. And some of it comes from blacks themselves, as middle-class blacks increasingly separate themselves from lower-class blacks. Despite court decisions, laws, and ordinances prohibiting racial discrimination and segregation, racial isolation persists as a prevalent pattern throughout the United States, especially in the metropolitan areas where more than two-thirds of the black population reside.

Lack of interaction across racial lines often results in the erroneous impression of calm and the absence of conflict. "There is nothing mysterious about this," a black psychologist said. "If the social, physical, and emotional distance between blacks and whites is large enough, they seldom reach across it to talk to each other." Thus it is common for whites and blacks to avoid activities that may lead to integration. The avoidance is easy when there is an unwillingness to see members of the other group as being trustworthy or deserving respect. People who live in racially homogeneous communities rarely question their isolation. What self-questioning they do is usually in the form of self-justification: "Why shouldn't whites (blacks) live among their own people. Blacks (whites) live together. It's a matter of comfort." Of course, this is not a rationalization if it is free choice, that is, if the alternative of living in racially desegregated neighborhoods is possible but both groups chose to not do it. That is seldom the case.

The term *race* is a wall between blacks and whites; the word preconditions them to be uncomfortable in the presence of each other. Because both parties are fearful of saying or doing inappropriate things and wish the contact to end as soon as possible, most black-white interactions tend to be staid and brief. But only through relaxed and long-term interactions will they be able to exorcise from themselves the angry and fearful forces which give rise to bigotry. Unfortunately, most white Americans have never spent a significant amount of time with a black American.

Failure in black-white relationships should not be perceived as a way of life, but as a challenge to be overcome. And the challenge is most likely to be met through face-to-face interactions. The race prejudice we find in neighborhoods, schools, and the workplace comes from the beliefs, values, and attitudes we learn from significant other people, like our parents. Although there exists no foolproof advice on how anyone can graciously come to terms with his or her racial prejudices, this book introduces positive steps toward shedding prejudice and learning to see one another—black and white—with greater understanding.

This book is not for people who devalue conciliatory approaches to social change. Nor is it for individuals looking for ways to circumvent civil rights laws, or for people who want to perpetuate tokenism. With eloquence that nearly matched her stage presence, Leontyne Price cautioned against white Americans who only wanted a few, talented black Americans to share our nation's social and economic bounties: "All token blacks have the same experience. I have been pointed to as a resolution to things that have not yet begun to be solved, because pointing to us token blacks eases the experience of millions [of white people], and this is dreadfully wrong" (Riley 1993, 65).

This is a book for people who, in spite of the current climate of mean-spiritedness, believe in cultural rapprochement between whites and blacks. Although racial and ethnic hatred is not solely a black-white issue, this book focuses on black-white problems because they are tearing America apart. The major objectives of this book, then, are (1) to educate the white reader about black American culture and black history, (2) to better understand the widening gap between the black middle and lower classes, (3) to gain a better sense of the school experience of black children, especially poor black children, and thereby learn how to teach these children more effectively, and (4) to be better informed and savvy about dealing with blacks in the workplace.

Fundamental to fostering positive black-white relations is knowing that sometimes white Americans and black

Americans not only speak different dialects, they also live in different physical and cultural environments. Because few white Americans know what life is like in black communities, even the best-intentioned white persons enter the black-white encounter grossly uninformed. Therefore, we will consider some of the differences between standard English and black English, between lower- and middle-class black Americans, inner-city and suburban blacks, affluence and poverty, and historical aspects of the black experience—conditions that continue to create cultural differences between white Americans and black Americans. Anecdotes, dialogues, critical incidents, excerpts from research findings, and poetry appear throughout the book in order to engage the reader in the black experience—from the inside looking out, as well as the outside looking in.

Because of their mark of oppression—race—high- and low-status blacks are often lumped together by whites. In order to help whites realize that black Americans are not an undifferentiated mass, this book provides a great deal of information about black heritage, culture, and class differences. It is not written to frighten or frustrate readers; rather, it is written to challenge them to seek ways to finish creating "one nation under God, indivisible, with liberty and justice for all." We must not continue to hurt each other emotionally or physically. To do so is national suicide. Black and white Americans both must learn to break the cycle of white superiority begetting black inferiority. Frantz Fanon (1967) pointed to the way out of this cycle several decades ago: "The only means of breaking this vicious cycle...is to restore to the other [black people], through mediation and recognition, [their] human reality.... Action from one side [whites] only would be useless, because what is to happen can only be brought about by the means of both [blacks and whites]...*they recognize themselves as mutually recognizing each other*" (217).

If housing, educational, and work patterns are predictive of change, there has been a modest shift in white attitudes toward black Americans. The willingness of a slowly growing number of whites to accept black (and other ethnic minority) families in their neighborhoods and schools reflects positive historical change. The major issue today is how to build on the readiness of large numbers of whites and blacks to learn, work, and live together. This book offers specific guidelines on how this goal can be pursued by individuals willing to seek a better understanding of each other and to work at developing communication and other human relations skills.

It is my wish that *Our Souls to Keep* will inspire others to write more on this subject. I also hope it will serve as an impetus to community action that focuses on ways all concerned Americans can join forces to finish the task of creating a nation that ensures liberty and justice for all its citizens. In essence, this book is about building sturdy cultural bridges.

"If I should die before I wake, I pray the Lord my soul to take," a child's prayer ends. Until we die, our mission, as I see it, is for white and black Americans to help keep each other's souls from being tarnished by ignorance, neglect, hatred, or indifference.

Part I

Black History and Culture

Chapter 1

Traditional African American Culture

African Americans are a difficult ethnic group to categorize, a difficulty which stems mainly from slavery, when African heritages were almost entirely lost through assimilation with non-African cultures. Consequently, it is not easy for some to think of African Americans as a heterogeneous people. Unlike most white Americans, who can be described in terms of their European culture of origin (German Americans, British Americans, Italian Americans, and French Americans), African Americans, who are a conglomeration of many cultures, are mainly characterized by their continent of origin. Slavery severed almost all genealogical ties. Thus Kenyan, Nigerian, Zambian, and other black African cultures are subsumed into a pan-African identity. This partly accounts for the African-style clothing and hairstyles black Americans have created to try to recapture a sense of their ethnic identities. The beliefs that black Americans hold about indigenous African people, blackness, and black culture are the foundation of their selfhood.

From the Inside, Looking Out:
An Autobiographical Statement

Too often the story of black-white relations consists of recollections of the harsh realities of slavery and too little mention of the socioeconomic gains that have been made. For many black Americans, it is difficult to separate problems that are caused by being descendants of slaves from those originating in being poor. Indeed, some black Americans have grown so used to defining their economic predicament in terms of slavery that any other reason would seem unusual. It is not so much the fact of being descendants of slaves that troubles them but the socioeconomic consequences of slavery. Race and poverty became intertwined, as the following autobiographical statement illustrates.

I grew up in the 1930s and 1940s in East Chicago, Indiana, a steel-mill town with a propensity for creating and sustaining slums. My subcommunity was called the Calumet. The other black subcommunities in East Chicago were the New Addition and the Harbor. In reality, each subcommunity was a rural Southern slum transplanted to a Northern urban outpost. The black residents were mainly from Alabama, Georgia, and Mississippi, having moved north during World War I to find better jobs. They spoke in southern dialects and passed on to their children the customs and traditions of the Old South. Indeed, "home" for these descendants of slaves remained their southern places of American origin, not East Chicago.

For all practical purposes, I lived in an urban plantation that was owned by white businessmen and controlled by their surrogates—politicians, realtors, police officers, teachers, social workers, storekeepers, and health care professionals. Initially, social customs and realtors rather than fences kept blacks out of white neighborhoods. Later, the police and white juvenile gangs kept us out. The neighborhoods where blacks and Hispanics lived were markedly inferior to the adjacent white neighborhoods. We lived in filth and squalor; most whites seemed to live in a relatively clean environment. Even poor white neighborhoods received better public services than our best neighborhoods.

The few affluent blacks who lived in East Chicago

formed their own bourgeois society, a subculture of black privilege. Those black Anglo-Saxons were *in* the community but not *of* it. Their children did not play with or socialize with poor folks like me. The first time I was called "nigger," the epithet came from an uppity black child, offended because I had touched her dress.

I lived in a series of unpainted shacks that lacked adequate insulation. Those structures were too hot in the summer and too cold in the winter. I almost always had a cold. Most of my homes did not have enough living space. Sometimes my mother, father, and I slept in a bed that was no more than an improved pallet. One shack had a hole in the floor for the toilet. Some shacks, including two that I lived in, did not have hot water and had only a woodstove for cooking. I bathed in tin tubs until I was eight years old. All the houses and, later, apartments I lived in had faulty plumbing and wiring. Many of the houses in the Calumet had dirt floors. One of my childhood dreams was to live in a "real," that is, structurally sound, house.

My mother often complained that our living condition had not greatly improved from what it had been in Hurstboro, Alabama. *But we were free!* That is, we were free except for the signs proclaiming "We Reserve the Right to Seat Our Customers" and "For Whites Only" that appeared in what we thought were public places. My parents had unknowingly fled from the racism of the South to the racism of the North. Years later the signs were removed, but the "conspiracy" by realtors to channel blacks into certain areas was not, and our housing choices were still greatly limited.

I remember the rats, bedbugs, and roaches that occupied every building in which I lived. They must have been mutant strains, because the insecticides and bug sprays my parents liberally dispensed were the bugs' appetizers; we were their main course. The DDT proved hazardous only to the health of people. I will never forget the rats, big and fearless—the kind that glare at you and dare you to take them on one-on-one. At night I played a game with the bedbugs. I would turn out the lights, lie still for about ten minutes, then quickly get up and turn on the lights. I would pull back the bedcovers, catch bedbugs running for a hole in the mattress, and squeeze them between my fingers until they popped and my blood oozed out of their crushed bodies. I still hate those bloodsuckers. And I still hate the slum dwellings where they thrive.

Almost all of the people in the Calumet ate the cheapest kinds of food as their main diet—chitterlings, pigs' knuckles, pigs' tails, pigs' feet, bacon ends, and greens. It wasn't called "soul food" then; it was basic survival food. At least twice a week my mother made meals of fatback, rice, and beans. I considered myself very fortunate. Unlike some of my friends, I periodically had fresh meat, milk, eggs, and fruit. I seldom had enough food, however. Most of my elementary and secondary school classmates were malnourished. And so was I.

People who lived in the Calumet were constantly exposed to health problems endemic to poor people—tooth decay, ear infections, poor eyesight, hypertension, smallpox, tetanus, and tuberculosis. Stillbirths and death at childbirth were commonplace. In fact, death in all forms was commonplace. Someone was always mourning the loss of a baby. Few physicians and dentists set up offices in the slums; we always had to travel great distances for meager health care.

Most homes had well-stocked medicine chests containing fever powders, quinine, toothache drops, and castor oil. My father was health-conscious—and, I thought at the time, sadistic. Four times a year—fall, winter, spring, and summer—he forced me to swallow two tablespoons of castor oil for medicinal reasons: to cleanse the inside of my body and to prevent colds. He was half right; I vomited and had diarrhea after each ordeal.

Few black families in East Chicago received adequate or regular medical care. I was nearsighted and needed corrective eyeglasses in elementary school. I got my first pair on June 12, 1950, a few days before my high school graduation. It was more important for my father to buy food and clothes than eyeglasses. Certainly, pulling my teeth himself rather than paying a dentist to fill them was economical and expedient. At the time I thought my parents were being mean to me. Now, of course, I realize that most of the health problems in the Calumet reflected parental poverty and ignorance, not lack of love.

The events of dying and death reminded us how alone we were and how vulnerable we were to being hurt. The harsh life of transient people—and most people were transients in the Calumet—gave a unique meaning to living. The church was the hub around which our community life revolved. For me there was something magical about the Baptist churches I attended. The choirs and preachers all seemed to make segregation and other oppression less harsh. They also made violence a less desirable alternative. In retrospect, I was brainwashed into believing that suffering had redemptive power.

It is difficult for individuals who are constantly praised to understand the drastic and devious steps the unpraised will take to be recognized. The bravado associated with being a social somebody, for example, led to great creativity among males in fighting, athletics, and making love. Girls fought for attention, too, also wanting to be recognized and appreciated. The jail was full of poor people with big egos. Our desire for winning had little to do with macho behavior; it had a lot to do with low self-esteem.

Unable to acquire the education needed for high-paying jobs, most black adults—including my parents—could only dream about working as something other than unskilled and semiskilled laborers in factories. After hours at the factories, my father cleaned white people's houses, and my mother nursed white children. Even blacks with college degrees were frequently underemployed and worked for lower wages than white high school dropouts.

Too many well-educated black people in my community were trapped in their ethnicity. Indeed, my community was a world of broken dreams and throwaway people.

At first, it was difficult for me to maintain a conviction to excel in school, where my dialect, now called black English, was considered inferior to standard English. As a child I said "tote" for *carry*, "chunk" for *throw*, "dis" for *this*, "fo" for *four*. Teachers in a Southern rural school would have understood me. In Northern urban schools my teachers not only misunderstood me but also made fun of my speech. I was an alien in my own country. (Later, I learned that many poor white people felt like that too.) People who speak different dialects and live in segregated neighborhoods do not live in the same cognitive world as that of affluent whites. My teachers' inability to understand this cultural phenomenon led most of them to label me "culturally deprived," "nonverbal," and "lacking motivation." Thus my elementary school classmates and I were labeled "failures," and most of us lived up to our labels. Fortunately, a few teachers cared enough about me to look beyond my poverty, Southern dialect, and low grades. With their help I became a high school graduate instead of a dropout—or pushout.

Sadly, a large number of black Americans who are growing up today have experiences similar to my own. These perplexing conditions are partly the residual effect of slavery and partly the result of low-income status. White Americans must understand the import of the autobiographical statement I make here. A "normal" lower-class black childhood means coping with distorted environmental and socioeconomic conditions that negatively shape the survivors' life views. It is not easy living in places researchers call "slums," "ghettos," or "inner cities"—culturally and physically circumscribed places that sometimes appear to be only slightly improved over pre-Civil War slave conditions.

The Specter of Slavery

Few subjects are more perplexing and irritating to well-intentioned white people than black Americans dredging up the events of early American history and the cruelties long suffered by blacks as reasons for their ethnic group's low levels of educational and economic achievement. Yet the pain has not diminished over the years. In the heat of discussions in which blacks inject slavery as a cause for today's racism, it is not unusual for white Americans to rebuke the black discussants with, "I'm tired of hearing about slavery. It ended before I was born. I never owned slaves. Furthermore, I refuse to accept responsibility for your people's lack of success. My ancestors suffered too when they came to America, but I don't try to blame anyone for it."

Occasionally this verbal confrontation ends when one or both parties acknowledge the importance and the truth of the other person's position. More often it ends, or is temporarily suspended, in a standoff or an unspoken truce that allows the individuals to move to other, less controversial topics. A common residual effect of this kind of verbal exchange is that whites come away thinking of blacks as whiners encapsulated in the past, historical cripples who use their ancestry as an excuse for their own shortcomings. And blacks label whites as racists—perpetuators of unequal educational and employment opportunities, inciters of crime, and arrogant power brokers. Thus, we have white people's truth and black people's truth. Somewhere between the two extremes is a truth that is neither white nor black.

It is difficult for most white Americans, especially those who believe that blacks and whites climbed out of slavery together, to understand the unwillingness of some blacks to let go of the horrors that characterized slavery in the United States.

For many African Americans, the issue of slavery is not

an excuse for their failures but a scale that allows them to measure white Americans' sensitivity to the many ways in which historical events have spawned and nurtured racism. Thus, the ghosts of slaves and the aftereffects of slavery test the strength of the bonds between blacks and whites. For other African Americans, the recounting of slavery is similar to Native Americans recalling the Trail of Tears or Jews recounting the Holocaust and is an effort to collect interest on a debt that cannot be fully paid. That debt can be acknowledged, however, with empathy, patience, and tangible support. Rejecting the notion of an unpaid debt, white conservatives often counter with the argument that the ledger has been balanced—indeed, over-balanced—through civil rights laws and affirmative action mandates. Even white liberals, while they do not trivialize the issue of slavery, tend to ask for forbearance; they wish that black Americans would just celebrate their "American" culture and stop being obsessed with their past. Although this is a reasonable desire, black culture must be considered in the context of its heritage, and that heritage is slavery and racism.

Nearly four hundred years of disparate community experiences have perpetuated differences between blacks and whites in housing, education, income, health care, and social class. Few whites are knowledgeable about the black experience, or about black American culture, which has been shaped by interaction with whites and, yes, by slavery. Consequently, the faces in the prism of black history are black and white.

Traditional African American Norms

While the lifestyles of black Americans vary by education, income, and geographical location, slavery and postslavery experiences have resulted in common black attitudes, values, beliefs, and behaviors that can be identified as *traditional African American norms (or culture)*. When culturally encapsulated would-be white friends and helpers assume that they can effectively interact with black Americans without understanding black cultural norms, values, and behavior, the result is usually a widening of the cultural gap and the raising of cultural barriers. The following information about black Americans should be considered basic knowledge for all white people.

Andrew Billingsley (1992) argues convincingly that the black American family is "an *intimate association* of persons of African descent who are *related to one another* by a variety of means, including blood, marriage, formal adoption, informal adoption, or by appropriation; sustained by a history of common residence in America; and deeply embedded in a network of social structures both internal to and external to itself" (28). Robert B. Hill (1977) was one of the first researchers to report that middle-income black Americans adopt children at a higher rate than their white counterparts. However, it is through informal adoption that many black children are cared for.

According to 1989 U.S. Census Bureau data, 1.2 million black children lived with a grandparent, usually a grandmother. However, the largest number of black children, one-third, lived in foster homes or with people who had no blood ties to them (Hill et al. 1989). A sizeable number of black Americans have what Carol Stack (1974) labeled "fictive kin" or "play kin." These mothers, fathers, brothers, sisters, grandparents, aunts, uncles, and cousins are not related by blood, but they assume role-appropriate behaviors to the individuals they "adopt." Fictive kin are called upon during emotional and financial crises, and they usually respond in a helpful way. Whatever their relationships, traditional black Americans have many characteristics in common, including those discussed in the remainder of this section.

Extended Family

The black American family is often maternally oriented (McAdoo 1988; Rodgers-Rose 1980), and the black extended family is a close-knit, interdependent group frequently consisting of grandparents, aunts, uncles, nieces, nephews, and cousins. Blood ties are the strongest bonds in black American culture. And, reflecting survival patterns from slavery, roles are interchanged within the black family more frequently than in most white families. The sharing of roles and jobs in the home stabilizes the family during crises.

Family members also share stories of previous generations. Storytellers within the black community are oral historians and educators. When they die, if they do not have a replacement, entire family histories disappear. It is as if a library has been destroyed. Camara Laye (1954) described the significance of storytellers he was exposed to: "I heard recalled the lofty deeds of my father's ancestors and their names from the earliest times. As the couplets were reeled off, it was like watching the growth of a great genealogical tree that spread its branches far and wide and flourished its boughs and twigs before my eyes" (32). Or in the words of Gayl Jones (1975): "My great-grandmama told my grandmama the part she lived through that my grandmama didn't live through and my grandmama told my mama what they both lived through and my mama told me what they all lived through and we were supposed to pass it down like that from generation to generation so we'd never forget" (9). Langston Hughes tells of this tradition in this poem:

> Aunt Sue has a head full of stories.
> Aunt Sue has a whole heart full of stories.
> Summer nights on the front porch
> Aunt Sue cuddles a brown-faced child to her bosom
> And tells him stories.
>
> Black slaves
> Working in the hot sun,
> And black slaves
> Walking in the dewy night,

And black slaves
Singing sorrow songs on the banks of the mighty river
Mingle themselves softly
In the flow of old Aunt Sue's voice,
Mingle themselves softly
In the dark shadows that cross and recross
Aunt Sue's stories.
And the dark-faced child listening,
Knows that Aunt Sue's stories are real stories.
He knows that Aunt Sue never got her stories
Out of any book at all,
But that they came
Right out of her own life.

The dark-faced child is quiet
Of a summer night
Listening to Aunt Sue's stories.
—"Aunt Sue's Stories"
Langston Hughes

Incidents of oppression are told to family members and friends, who in turn share them with others. Eventually, the listeners begin to realize that these stories are not unique incidents but rather a pattern of white abusers and black victims. Consequently, when one black person is abused by whites, other blacks retrieve from their memory similar abuses, thereby reinforcing group ties. Thus, when talking about themselves and other family members, they use the personal pronoun "we." For example, a white male supervisor was confused by a black female subordinate's grievance: "We're tired of being treated like this."

"Who else is complaining about this?" he asked.

"I'm talking about me," she snapped. The reference was to her situation, but she was at the same time remembering and reacting to stories that relatives told of similar experiences, and without realizing it, she was speaking for them too.

In addition to being the foremost storytellers, grandparents perform many other useful community services.

In many families they are the baby-sitters of choice because they are concerned for their grandchildren's welfare and are more dependable than caregivers outside the family. It is common for grandparents to have tacit permission to chastise any misbehaving black child, family member or otherwise. And if the parents are told about the child's behavior, they will mete out additional punishment. By words and facial expression, black adults will admonish children who are disrespectful to their grandparents: "Hug your grandparents and say 'I'm sorry' and also say 'Thank you for making it possible for me and my parents to have life.'"

The traditional black family has produced generation after generation of people who have given each other racial identity, connection, and succor. The song "We Are Family" has broad meaning for most blacks and special meaning for kinfolks.

Kinship Bonds

Children belong to the community, and all adults are responsible for their upbringing. While it has lessened in the last decade, the belief still holds that it takes an entire community to raise a child. Children born in and out of wedlock are loved (McAdoo and McAdoo 1985; Thompson 1974). *Illegitimacy* is not a term tradition-oriented blacks use to describe children born out of wedlock. The term refers to parents and has little to do with acceptance of children, who are proof of an individual's manhood or womanhood. And caring for children is proof of an individual's humanity. When children reach adulthood, they leave home. Children born in wedlock (more than those born out of wedlock) often settle close to their parents or other relatives. Elder family members are sources of support and advice. Family unity, loyalty, and cooperation are part of the traditional black American lifestyle to the point that siblings are more important than marital partners or friends. For example, when forced to choose between his wife or his sibling, the traditional black man would probably choose his sibling; black women tend to make similar choices. "People fall in and out of love with other people; they must always love their brothers and sisters," a black seamstress explained. "Blood is thicker than water."

Kinship bonds play a major role in black-white cross-cultural differentiation. Compared with white families, black sibling relationships are more interdependent and loyal (Gold 1990; Hecht et al. 1993; Woods 1994). Also, black siblings usually describe their childhood and adulthood together as "tight" [close] interactions that are mutually supportive. For example, black brothers and sisters assume an active role in helping to rear their siblings' children and expect from each other an equitable distribution of time and resources in caring for each other and for infirm parents, grandparents, and other family members. In other words, black families become self-sustaining microcommunities. In the vernacular of the community, they are "there for each other."

Some white Americans are perplexed, even annoyed, when a sibling intercedes on behalf of his or her sister or brother without having any formal status in the situation at hand. A white plant supervisor, for example, got a first-hand glimpse of this when a black employee's sister, whom he had never met, called to complain about the harsh treatment her sister was receiving on the job. On another occasion, in her eulogy for James Baldwin in 1988 at the Cathedral of St. John the Divine in New York City, Maya Angelou described the importance of black brothers to their sisters: "Black women may find lovers on street corners and even in church pews, but brothers are hard to come by and are as necessary as air and as precious as love. Black women in this desolate world, black women in this cruel time have a crying need for brothers."

The importance of the mother in the black family is illustrated by a mild-mannered black teenager who thus cautioned a friend: "If you say my old man [father] is a dirty bastard, I might just laugh. But if you say my mom is a no-good bitch, I'll kick your ass. Nobody talk that way about my mom." Derogatory statements about a black American's mother are crushing blows, not only because she is "Mother" but also because she is often the only significant parent in the home. Mothers or mother surrogates, including grandmothers, oldest daughters, and aunts, are the primary stabilizers in the black American family.

In spite of their general absence, some black fathers are well thought of by their children. Marva N. Collins's (1986) description of her father is an example:

> He is not listed in the history books. Few people have heard of him, and no front-page stories heralded his demise, but I shall always remember that it was he who influenced my life. His name will not matter to most readers because...he never made the "Ten Most Admired" list. But in my book, he is the greatest man I have ever known (105).

Within the black community it would be wrong to dismiss black fathers as being irrelevant to the black family. And it would also be wrong not to chastise them when they neglect their parental responsibilities.

Single-parent households are growing (nearly 50 percent), especially young mothers living alone with their elderly parents. This situation, a relatively recent phenomenon among black Americans (Sudarkasa 1993), is discussed a lot today. Homes headed by black mothers have been cited as the major reason why a disproportionate number of blacks are mired in poverty. Whether middle class or lower class, the ideal black family still consists of a mother, a father, and a child or children. Nevertheless, the data are alarming.

The precarious state of the institution of marriage in the black community is seen in 1996 National Center for Health Statistics data: seventy percent of black children were born out of wedlock, and almost 50 percent of black mothers were never married. Twenty-two percent of never-married black mothers (about 10 percent adoptive parents) had incomes above $75,000, however, clear evidence that out-of-wedlock births are not solely a lower-class phenomenon. A staggering number of black children learn to deal with the fact that they live in a female-dominated home.

Some of the tension centering on single-parent homes is relieved through verbal assault on another's parentage, an activity that is sometimes referred to as "playing the dozens." The objective is to insult one's opponent without showing anger when he or she responds. The "winner" is the individual who scores the most points through insults that are not effectively countered. Any player who resorts to physical aggression immediately loses. A game of the dozens may go like this:

> Mark: Come here, son.
> Gene: I ain't yo son, I'm yo daddy.
> Mark: Oh! You wanna get down and play the dozens, huh? Listen son. I don't play the dozens cause the dozens is bad, but I can tell you how many children yo mammy had. She didn't have one, she didn't have two, she had twenty-nine bulldogs just like you.
> Gene: Now, son, is that any way for you to talk to yo daddy? You keep talking like that and I'm gonna tell everybody what color drawers yo mama wear.

This verbal game, while it may seem vulgar or cruel to an outsider, allows black community members to adjust to absent fathers or to not knowing who their father is. In some ways, this is a form of steeling children to embarrassing information.

Childhood in the black American community revolves around assertive behavior and challenges to authority (Hale 1982; Thompson 1974). Through the constant crossing of wills, children learn acceptable limits of their behavior. Discipline is often strict, harsh, and preoccupied with teaching children respect for their elders, respect for authority, responsibility for themselves, and an understanding of what it means to be black in the United States. In earlier times, as a sign of respect, children were taught not to look adults in the eye and to say "Yes, sir" and "No, ma'am" when answering them. Adults, however, did look at children when talking to them; thus the subordinate-superior relationship was established.

Black English and Communication

Black English is the dialect spoken by many black Americans (Anderson 1994; Dillard 1975; Seymour 1972). In 1982 the American Speech-Language-Hearing Association classified black English (or "Ebonics," as it has recently been called) as a separate dialect. The syntax, pronunciation, inflection, verb usage, and verb enhancers are culturally established conventions that are different from standard (white) English. Derived from standard English and some elements of the slaves' African languages centuries ago, black English is not debased or bad English. It is a dialect with a structure and a form of its own. For example, the verb *to be* is not extensively conjugated: "I be late tomorrow." Also, a double negative expressed in black English is as logical as the French negative in the double form (*ne...pas*): "I didn't have no money." Consider a black speaker's explanation: "White people might not have any money but I didn't have a penny, a credit card—*nothing*. I didn't have no money!" This conveys the desperate nature of the situation. Similarly, the singer who croons "I can't get any satisfaction" is less persuasive in the black community than one who sings "I can't get no satisfaction."

> There is increasing evidence that the differences of Afro speech from Anglo speech are mainly due to the survival of characteristics of African languages among black people in America. For instance, the *th* sound is absent in many West African languages, so many Afros substitute *d* as in *de book* or *dis* or *dat....* Another example of some differences between Afro

dialect and standard English dialect is the tendency to drop final consonants, like *ed*, *s*, or *t*. So you might hear *tes* for *test* or *col* for *cold*. In some cases, the final *th* becomes *f*, as in *oaf* for *oath* or *bof* for *both*. The *r* in *store* or *door* might be left out, so you hear *sto* or *do*.

Afro dialect finds uses for double and multiple negatives, usually for emphasis. "You ain't gone find me at no touchie-feelie sensitivity session at no time soon!" Still another interesting characteristic of Afro dialect has no counterpart in "standard" English: The use of the verb *to be* in a continuous present tense. Thus, "She be scheming" means she schemed in the past, is probably scheming now, and will most likely be scheming in the future (Taylor 1976, 1-2).

Black English is also characterized as being very expressive and making creative use of silent language or nonverbal communication, technically called *kinesthetics*. When gestures, posture, vocal intonations, and facial expressions are correctly interpreted, a few words can convey an entire story.

In 1996, desperately seeking a way to better educate some of their low-achieving black students, the Oakland, California, public schools passed a resolution declaring Ebonics a second language and requiring teacher and parent training in black English language patterns. The public backlash, particularly from black Americans, was swift and acrimonious. Critics accused the school board of insulting black students' intelligence and lowering educational standards by teaching black English. Not so, school board president Lucilla Harrison responded. "We're not going to glorify black English. But we're not going to devalue children who use it" (Puente 1996, 3A).

It is true that a sizable number (but not the majority) of black children speak black English. And it is also true that in order to be able to communicate with those students, teachers should understand the dialect. But it is unlikely that designating Ebonics a "language" will significantly improve the quality of education for black students, who must master standard English if they are to be successful. Some black Americans joke about being bilingual in black English and white (standard) English. Acceptance and even survival in some black neighborhoods depends on being able to speak black English. The black person who speaks "proper" (standard) English is suspect and is likely to be looked on as being a snob. Even so, success in the larger community, including school and the workplace, requires proficiency in standard English. Therefore, most blacks who live in such neighborhoods also become fluent in standard English. The majority of individuals (blacks and whites) who do not speak black English demean those who do and judge it as substandard or bad English. Culturally enlightened people, however, know that black English is neither worse nor better than standard English; it is merely different.

Male Demeanor and Black Rage

An important aspect of black American culture is the perceived proper behavior of black males (Hare and Hare 1984; Wallace 1979). Sometimes referred to as "being cool," this behavior requires black males to avoid self-disclosure through words or gestures. Expressing feelings is viewed as a sign of weakness or a loss of will and indicates a lack of pride. This front-stage cool behavior becomes backstage behavior too. Black males seldom let their guard down—even around people who care about them. This masking of feelings shuts out family, friends, and foes and often causes white writers to describe black American males as unconcerned, aloof, emotionless, or fearless instead of strong, suave, or debonair (as black males would interpret the behavior).

Such emotional separation from other people is a survival technique. Without the ability to hide their emotions, many black males would find the world overwhelming. The well-trimmed hair; the slow, swaggering walk; and the boisterous conversations are examples of an extreme "coolness" that seeks to hide an existence continuously threatened with cultural extinction (Majors and Billson 1993). *Braggadocio* is a common form of communication among black males, especially teenagers and young adults. According to their self-reports, they can outfight, outsmart, and outlove their peers. In black talk, they are bad (excellent, great), bodacious (superb), def (great), in there (good-looking).

In community statistics, however, a disproportionate number of black males are at risk: plagued with hypertension; killed by knives, guns, and drugs; and mocked by their inability to kick butt (to excel at something). Getting the basics for survival—food, shelter, and clothing—dwarfs other concerns. Darwinian-like, only the strong survive.

Keeping one's cool creates an atmosphere fertile for the growth and development of urban nomads who are less vulnerable to disillusionment. Moving from community to community and trying not to know the people in their present neighborhood or remember those in their previous neighborhood cause some black males to withdraw into themselves. For most of them, though, the coolness is only skin deep. In the words of a black youth: "You just can't let a friend or even a stranger starve to death...even if it means sharing your last piece of bread with him.... You got to help less fortunate people...especially brothers [other black males]."

The inordinate stress of being both black and male, particularly if one lives in an inner city, can be seen in suicide rates. In 1994, for example, suicide was the third leading killer of African American males ages 15 to 24, exceeded only by homicide and accidents. From 1980 to 1994, according to U.S. Department of Health and Human Services data, the suicide rate among black males ages 10 to 14 quadrupled (from .52 to 2.13 per 100,000 people); among black males ages 15 to 19, it tripled (from 5.6 to 16.6); and among black males ages 20 to 24, it increased one-fourth (from 19.9 to 24.8). Although mental health practitioners and social scientists are not sure why these increases have occurred, it is evident that (1) sometimes when black males lose their cool, they also lose their desire to live, (2) as a whole, black males handle stress less well than black females, and (3) increases in black male suicide rates are significantly higher than those of any other racial group.

A cultural by-product of slavery is African American males' reluctance to let white people see their anger. Or, as Toni Morrison wrote, "When a man angers you, he conquers you" (Riley 1993, 20). But the calm veneer often masks rage and when released, it can be as blinding as the rage Maya Angelou described: "I always knew that fury was my natural enemy. It clotted my blood and clogged my pores. It literally blinded me so that I lost my peripheral vision" (Riley 1993, 20). There is a general feeling among black Americans that they must wear a pleasant mask when around white people; thus, they laugh and sing in order to mask their rage, as recounted by Paul Laurence Dunbar.

> We wear the mask that grins and lies,
> It hides our cheeks and shades our eyes,—
> This debt we pay to human guile;
> With torn and bleeding hearts we smile,
> And mouth with myriad subtleties.
>
> Why should the world be overwise,
> In counting all our tears and sighs?
> Nay, let them only see us, while
>   We wear the mask.
>
> We smile, but, O great Christ, our cries
> To Thee from tortured souls arise.
> We sing, but oh, the clay is vile
> Beneath our feet, and long the mile;
> But let the world dream otherwise,
>   We wear the mask.
>
>   —"We Wear the Mask"
>   Paul Laurence Dunbar

Each individual, however, can tolerate only so much anger without exploding. In black-white relationships this explosion often takes the form of cruel words that can imperil or destroy friendships. And violence of words can lead to violence of action. This breaks the code of subservient behavior that blacks learn: there is a proper time to speak to whites, a correct tone of voice to be used, and appropriate words to be spoken. If white people are physically touched, it should be in a way that conveys respect. Subservient or not, most blacks learn not to be easily convinced by what whites tell them. Their disdain for whites, however, is almost always expressed through contemptuous looks and insulting words rather than physical aggression.

Religious Orientation

As a whole, black Americans are deeply religious (Costen 1993; J. R. Washington Jr. 1994). Their spirituality is reinforced through common history and life experiences and Afrocentric ideals centering on family unity. Richard Wright (1941) noted that the church is the door through which black Americans first walked into Western civilization. Religious services for slaves in America are where they were first allowed to express their personalities. The black Protestant church became not merely the means through which Western thought from ancient Greeks to twentieth-century existentialists entered directly into the intellectual experience of black people, but it also offered a common spiritual, economic, and political experience. Consequently, the black church has historically been a major source of education, inspiration, and liberation.

The church offers spiritual hope to many persons who live in oppressive environments. It is in the church group where some black Americans get their only feeling of belonging to a community. And they frequently define their belonging in terms of suffering. They may appear to outsiders to be a group of complainers who meet to share each other's misery, but, in reality, they meet to muster enough energy and faith to continue living. This is stated in the sentiment, "We are a fellowship of sufferers."

The premises of most black denominations—we are poor people, but we can have a mansion in heaven; we are a fellowship of sufferers—can be rationalized by church members as preconditions for salvation. Indeed, a deep pride in suffering is instilled in the faithful. This is not to imply that there is a religious scheme to keep black people impoverished. Rather, it implies that these religious sentiments help individuals to cope with being poor. When all else seems lost, getting on their knees and saying "amen" makes some black people feel better, even if it is for only a brief time.

The church also offers a facility for conducting community meetings and other activities. Black churches are involved in a myriad of community outreach activities: senior citizen housing, parenting programs, low-income housing, food and clothing programs, alcohol and drug counseling, day-care centers, G.E.D. preparation, homeless shelters, youth programs, and AIDS education (Billingsley 1992; Billingsley and Caldwell 1991; Mukenge 1983). These church activities lessen the effects of unstable work situations and an absence of any other organized community life.

Religious services tend to be spontaneous and lively with congregation-wide participation, services so moving that Clarence Reed was inspired to write:

Forever let there be shouting Sisters,
"Oh yes"
Shouting joyous exalting shouts
"Yes Lord!"
Voices massed, husky-throated, buxom
Brown sisters shouting,
Oh praise be life and living
O dead don't squirm
They mourn for you too with glad heart

That you have lived
Sprung from their loins
Shimmering blue-black in the sun,
Sucked in life, spit out joy,
Laughed to manhood,
Shouted in hell,
Went down to death with a
rhapsodic moan
Oh, shout, Sister, shout
Sing me along with clapping hands
And heal my heart
Echoing tamborines in my soul
"Oh yes Lord"
There is no more to God than you
Giver,
Sustainer
Joyous Sister shouting....
—"In a Harlem Store Front Church"
Clarence Reed

A free expression of feelings is a characteristic behavior in most black churches. In revivals one will witness mass wailing and crying. During the sermon, which is usually long and highly emotional, the audience participates through the utterance of emotional "amens." Songs are sung with the fullest possible emotional commitment, often with tears.

Within the context of Christian tenets, black ministers teach their followers to put aside bigotry and use nonviolent behavior to counter racism. A black mother said, "My pastor teaches us that there's no place in God's world for hate. No matter what white folks do to us, we gotta forgive them. The eye-for-an-eye approach will only get people dead. It won't get us to Heaven."

Folk Medicine

Every medical system is based on ideas about survival and about what constitutes health and what constitutes illness. Folk health systems are frequently called "strange" or "weird" by individuals who are unfamiliar with them. What is strange and what is not depends on familiarity. These kinds of health practices are common in less developed or Third-World countries, but they are not strange once one becomes familiar with them. However, it is important to note that to become familiar with something does not require an individual to accept it as part of his or her own way of life.

Third-World peoples are not as likely as others to separate mental and physical aspects of health into mind-body dichotomies. Third-World medical beliefs are holistic and can be subsumed under three foci: magic, religion, and witchcraft. For example, the belief in magic leads to assumptions that disease is the result of human behavior and that the cure is achieved by sorcery. A religious orientation toward the world lends itself to assumptions that disease is the result of supernatural forces and that cures can be found by successfully appealing to supernatural forces. A scientific view, on the other hand, leads to the assumption that ill health—physical and mental—is the result of cause-effect relations of natural phenomena, and the cure is achieved by scientific intervention.

African health practices make little distinction between physicians and mental health practitioners; both attend to the physical, emotional, and spiritual health of the people (Carothers 1970). In adopting a holistic approach to health care, tradition-oriented black Americans believe the sick person is a biological, psychosocial, and spiritual whole being. According to traditional African beliefs, both living and dead things influence an individual's health. In addition, health is directly related to nature. To be in harmony with nature is to have good health, whereas illness reflects disharmony with nature. The secret to good health among many black Americans is maintaining a balance between the forces of good and evil. In some communities, for example, voodoo doctors or conjurers are summoned to cast out evil spirits or demons. Several methods—including putting pins in dolls and applying heat and cold to an afflicted person's body—have been carried over from ancient African custom. Extensive use is made of roots, minerals, and plant mixtures. Faith healers, root doctors, and spiritualists are still consulted in some black communities. However, like other ethnic groups, as black Americans become middle class, they abandon folk cures, utilizing modern health facilities instead.

Black Americans with extremely low income use free clinical health services when pain, bleeding, fever, or symptoms seem life-threatening and they cannot get relief from home remedies such as castor oil and goose-grease plasters and wrapping an individual's chest in ointment-treated flannel. When members of religious congregations are sick at home or in a hospital, it is common for other members to "visit in small groups (missionary circles, brotherhood members, Sunday school classes, choir members, and so forth). These visits reinforce a sense of individual importance and personhood. The sessions may include prayer, singing, and religious readings" (Thomas 1981, 216).

Acculturation

As more and more African Americans internalize middle-class white cultural beliefs and norms, the number of tradition-oriented black Americans has diminished. Even though there are relatively few "pure" tradition-oriented black Americans, many vestiges of the old culture remain, particularly among individuals who have been denied access to mainstream American society. In terms of age, most of today's tradition-oriented blacks were born before 1960. But a sizable number of younger blacks also adhere to some of the traditional beliefs, values, and behaviors. Ways of life disappear slowly—and never, if one person in the family passes them on to the next generation.

It is important to note that African Americans and Southern whites are culturally more alike than different. Indeed, the symbiosis that occurred during the pre-Civil

War period did not merely create miscegenation between the races, it fused lifestyles. Whereas Southern whites as a whole have had considerable opportunities to learn new ways of life, fewer blacks have been so privileged. The search for a positive self-identity, which is the subject of the next chapter, determines whether they hold on to traditional ways of life, adopt nontraditional ones, or blend the two.

Chapter 2

Search for Identity: A Dream Deferred

The United States is a nation of tremendous promise. Respect for cultural differences and opportunities for all citizens to be well educated, to realize their full economic potential, and to find a suitable place in society according to their abilities and efforts are central premises of our democracy. Some disgruntled blacks argue that democracy is merely a rug under which hateful whites sweep their oppressive practices. However the notion is stated, the main point is that most black Americans have yet to be treated like first-class citizens. Thus, the full benefit of citizenship is a dream that has been deferred. Perhaps, as Langston Hughes wrote, the dream will be realized tomorrow.

I, too, sing America.
I am the darker brother.
They send me to eat in the kitchen
When company comes,
But I laugh,
And eat well,
And grow strong.

Tomorrow,
I'll be at the table
When company comes.
Nobody'll dare
Say to me,

"Eat in the kitchen,"
Then.

Besides,
They'll see how beautiful I am
And be ashamed—
I, too, am America.

—"I, Too"
Langston Hughes

Multicultural Family Members

This quest for acceptance is not, as some white people believe, a struggle between distinct racial groups. There *are* no pure races in the United States. To the contrary, more often than not the struggle is a confrontation among distant relatives. In reality, this family matter is neither black nor white. The breaking up of black families and wanton sexual activities of white males during the years of slavery were not without effect on white families. Clear physical distinctions between Negroes and Caucasians became permanently blurred through miscegenation. The differing skin colors of black Americans are living proof of these liaisons, mainly between white men and black women during the seventeenth, eighteenth, and nineteenth centuries. Another poem by Langston Hughes vividly captures the blurring of lines between black and white Americans.

My old man's a white old man
and my old mother's black.
If ever I cursed my white old man
I take my curses back.

If ever I cursed my black old mother
and wished she were in hell,
I'm sorry for that evil wish
And now I wish her well.

My old man died in a fine big house.
My ma died in a shack.

I wonder where I'm gonna die,
Being neither white nor black?

—"Cross"
Langston Hughes

That white people are prejudiced against blacks and reject them because of skin shade is well known, but what is often not such common knowledge is that color bigotry comes not only from whites but from blacks as well. Countless black Americans in the early twentieth century spent a major portion of their waking hours yearning and trying to become white. All blacks—the educated, the illiterate, the strong, and the weak—were constantly reminded of their inferiority. The stigma of blackness could not be washed away with platitudes. Black Americans learned the lesson well, too well. They believed that black was ugly, something to be ashamed of. This rhyme that many black Americans learned in childhood captured such self-degradation:

If you're white, you're right.
If you're brown, stick around.
If you're yellow, you're mellow.
If you're black, get back.

Skin colors of black Americans come in many different shades. There are black, dark brown, brown, light brown, and white hues. These various colors have inspired descriptive words to differentiate them: deep chocolate, cinnamon brown, honey, peach, vanilla. There are also colors that blacks use to denigrate themselves, including redbone and high yellow.

A light-skinned black American university student described her plight when going out dancing with darker-skinned friends:

> I remember an occasion as an adult when I and a group of other women were going out to a nightclub. One of the women commented that because I was in the group, none of the other women would get to dance because "you know how all the fellas like 'redbones.'" What is really striking about this

comment is not simply that the woman had a problem with my light skin, but rather that she felt comfortable using the [derogatory] term in my presence and felt that I had no reason to be insulted by it....
Darker-skinned blacks, in my opinion, sometimes tend to feel that they have been victimized so much by other people's preference for light skin that they have free reign when it comes to light-skinned African Americans. It's as if I should apologize for my complexion.

Although it still exists, there at least appears to be a lessening of color prejudice among African Americans. As they travel throughout the world, black Americans are realizing that white people come in different shades too—as many shades as black people. Then the reality starts setting in. The only race of any significance is the human race, not one defined in terms of skin pigmentation.

Black Identity

There are familiar responses black Americans give to nonblacks who ask "What's it like to be a black American?" One answer is, "If you have to ask, you'll never know." More descriptive answers from those who have experienced overtly racist behaviors are "It's hell" or "It's pain." Not all black Americans feel this way, but many of them have had moments when they have been tempted to disavow all that is black. W. E. B. Du Bois (1903) described the black American experience as that of a "twoness," a "double-consciousness":

It is a peculiar sensation, this double-consciousness, this sense of always looking at one's self through the eyes of others, of measuring one's soul by the tape of a world that looks on in amused contempt and pity. One ever feels his twoness—an American, a Negro, two souls, two thoughts, two unreconciled strivings; two warring ideals in one dark body, whose dogged strength alone keeps it from being torn asunder (1965, 215).

Most Americans, white and black, either consciously or subconsciously, have long identified the color black as the symbolic antonym of white. More often than not, whiteness has been associated with everything that was good—Christ and the angels, cleanliness, and virtue—and black, with all that was bad. One can find the contrasts in dictionaries, ranging from "white hope" to "whitewash," from "blackball" to "blackmail."

A review of literature reveals that at various times black has stood for dirt, sin, and the devil. The metaphorical use of "black as evil" and "white as good" is abundant throughout the Bible. These usages presage privilege or privation. In fact, the Bible's central theme of good (light) and evil (darkness) has been a chief source of reference for racial bigots, as illustrated by the Imperial Instructions of the Ku Klux Klan: "Every Klansman should read [the Bible] the first thing every morning and endeavor to live by it during the day." Shakespeare adopted similar imagery. In *Love's Labour's Lost* the King of Navarre says: "O paradox! Black is the badge of hell. The hue of dungeons and the scowl of night." In yet another scornful tone Shakespeare had Macbeth cry out to a servant: "The devil damn thee black...!" Both utterances illustrate the symbolic joining of evil and blackness. Such examples in both theology and literature are endless.

Beginning with slavery, the elevation of the color white and the debasement of black have been etched deep in the minds of Americans, and most whites have more or less unconsciously taken it as nourishment for their own self-esteem. An American of mixed "white" and "black" blood, no matter how small the percentage (one drop), is considered black by the general public. Like the English child in one of William Blake's poems, white Americans were already the color of angels, while blacks could only yearn after whiteness, whether of character, soul, or skin, and hope that by becoming "like" white people, they would be loved. James Baldwin (1961) described the tragic poignancy of such hope:

> At home one's hair was always being attacked with hard brushes and combs and Vaseline; it was shameful to have "nappy" hair.... One was always being mercilessly scrubbed and polished as though in hope that a stain could thus be washed away.... The women were forever straightening and curling their hair, and using bleaching creams. And yet, it was clear that none of this would release one from the stigma of being a Negro; this effort merely increased the shame and rage. There was not, no matter where one turned, any acceptable image of oneself, no proof of one's existence. One had the choice, either, of "acting just like a nigger" or of not acting just like a nigger and only those who have tried it know how impossible it is to tell the difference (73).

By 1963, a few black leaders had begun to emphasize the need to strengthen black identity, and a growing number of black Americans began to decide not to let other people's fixation with color immobilize them. It was clear to these blacks that they would not, as Dudley Randall wrote, fit "The Melting Pot," nor did they want to any longer.

> There is a magic melting pot
> where any girl or man
> can step in Czech or Greek or Scot,
> step out American.
>
> **Johann** and **Jan** and **Jean** and **Juan**,
> **Giovanni** and **Ivan**
> step in and then step out again
> all freshly christened **John**.
>
> Sam, watching, said, "Why, I was here
> even before they came,"
> and stepped in too, but was tossed out
> before he passed the brim.

And every time Sam tried that pot
they threw him out again.
"Keep out. This is our private pot.
We don't want your black stain."

At last, thrown out a thousand times,
Sam said, "I don't give a damn.
Shove your old pot. You can like it or not,
but I'll be just what I am."
—"The Melting Pot"
Dudley Randall

And being "just what I am" is the soul-rending process
black Americans experience in discovering and becoming
proud of their ethnic group's place in America; intellectual and emotional rapprochement between black and
white Americans is likely to occur only when whites begin
to grasp this painful search. This kind of self-discovery is
puzzling for white Americans, whose identity is already
firmly anchored in mainstream American culture. They
do not have to resort to slogans such as "white is beautiful" to bolster their self-image. A once-popular song begins, "You're so vain, I bet you think this song is about
you." Countless white Americans are so vain that they
think black Americans' search for positive self-identity is
about whites. Usually it is not. Rather, it is about accepting oneself, not about resenting white people. That is, black
Americans must accept themselves, whether they have light
or dark skin, an aquiline or flat nose, straight or curly
hair, light or dark eyes.

The closest black Americans can come to explaining
this quest for identity and self-acceptance to white people
is to describe it in terms of discovering one's blackness
and loving it: black *is* beautiful. As if overcome by a warm
flash of insight, this experience is exhilarating. It is also
novel for people who have lost or never had the experience of feeling good about their ethnicity. This is especially important for black females, who seem devalued by

media standards of beauty (which, by the way, also de-value most white females): thinness, certain hair texture, and a narrow range of facial features.

Equally gratifying is discovering the beauty of other black peoples throughout the world. White Americans who do not understand this kind of ethnicity rapprochement may be able to do so after answering the following questions: have you ever been unhappy with your body image—its size, shape, weight, or color? If so, what emotions did you feel—inferiority, inadequacy, or unattractiveness? All of these are compounded by an ethnic inferiority complex.

Black pride is about black people redefining themselves, and only they can do it. It is discovering and reclaiming their history in order to create a sense of black community and togetherness. For many people of African heritage this process begins with terminology (Americans of African descent have had a series of aliases—*Negro, colored, black, Afro-American*), accepting the terms *black* or *African American* and rejecting *Negro* because it was given to them by white Americans (Fairchild 1985).

White Americans have played their own role in the terminology debate. They ask why blacks call themselves "African" Americans rather than just Americans. But the question is sophistic. The relevant question is, "Do most white Americans believe that black Americans are the same as they are and must receive equal rights and privileges?" For example, white mobs have not lynched "Americans," they've lynched "niggers" and "coons." Cowardly whites have not burned "American" churches, they have burned black churches. Blacks are criticized, sometimes punished, by whites for setting themselves apart from other Americans by calling themselves African Americans; yet, they are ridiculed or ostracized by whites when they call themselves simply Americans and try to get the same rights and privileges most whites have. This is a classic catch-22 situation in which race matters (West 1993).

Black History Revisited

Although not all black Americans believe that terminology is particularly important, almost all of them acknowledge the need to learn black history. It is important therefore for white Americans to have a knowledge of black history as well, especially if they are to counter stereotypes and myths.

Most Americans think of early historical contributions to the United States by black Americans as being almost exclusively in their roles as slaves. In fact, numerous cultural contributions were made by both slaves and free persons (Brodie 1993; Ploski and Williams 1992):

- Estevanico, an African with the Spanish explorers, who traveled to the Arizona and New Mexico territories in 1538
- Phillis Wheatley, a slave in the 1760s, who wrote poetry that was praised throughout the world
- Jean Point du Sable, a black trader, who founded a settlement that grew into Chicago
- Peter Salem, a distinguished black soldier, who fought in the battles of Lexington, Concord, and Bunker Hill
- Five thousand slaves and free blacks who served in the Continental Army and Navy between 1776 and 1781
- Black abolitionists, including Frederick Douglass and Sojourner Truth
- Rebel slaves Denmark Vessey, Gabriel Prosser, and Nat Turner, who powerfully advanced the cause of Emancipation
- George W. Bush, a black scout, who led white settlers into the Oregon Territory in 1844
- Norbert Rillieux, who, in 1846, invented the vacuum pan that revolutionized the sugar-refining industry
- Lewis Temple, of Massachusetts, who invented the toggle harpoon in 1848
- James Beckwourth, born a slave, who discovered an important pass through the Sierra Nevada in 1850

- John M. Langston, of Ohio, who in 1855 became the first black elected to a political office in the United States
- Thirteen of the fourteen jockeys who rode in the first Kentucky Derby in 1875
- Jan Matzeliger, who in 1883 invented the first machine that manufactured an entire shoe
- Dr. Daniel Hale Williams, who, in 1893, performed the first successful open-heart operation in the United States
- Andrew J. Beard, born a slave, who, in 1897, invented the automatic railroad coupler, also known as the Jenny Coupler
- Matthew Henson, who accompanied Commander Robert E. Peary on his North Pole expedition in 1909
- Garrett A. Morgan, who invented the automatic traffic light in 1923
- Marian Anderson, who, denied a Washington auditorium in 1939, sang before 75,000 people at the Lincoln Memorial (Eleanor Roosevelt made that possible)
- Dr. Charles Drew, who developed a blood transfusion process—and died in 1941 because a white hospital refused to give him a transfusion
- Dorie Miller, who shot down four Japanese planes at Pearl Harbor in 1941, thus becoming the first American hero of World War II

Almost all aspects of modern-day America have been influenced directly or indirectly by the contributions of black Americans. Their recent achievements are built on the success of the earlier contributors. For instance, in the realm of music America is indebted to James Bland for composing "Carry Me Back to Old Virginny," the former official state song of Virginia. William C. Handy's "Saint Louis Blues" is a masterpiece of the blues genre. "Ma" (Gertrude Pridgett) Rainey is best known as the "Mother of the Blues," followed by Bessie Smith, another founding mother of the blues. William Grant Still's "Afro-American Symphony" is a symphonic masterpiece, as is Howard Swanson's "Short Symphony" that was recorded by conductor Dimitri Mitropoulos. Sissieri Jones, Marian Anderson (the first black singer to perform at the Metropolitan Opera in a leading role), Paul Robeson, Roland Hayes, and Dorothy Maynor were world-acclaimed concert and opera singers. Leontyne Price was the first black opera singer to achieve worldwide status as "prima donna assoluta." Singer and actress Lena Horne starred in the longest-running one-woman Broadway show. Katherine Dunham and Pearl Primus introduced Caribbean and African dances to American audiences. Harry Burleigh, R. Nathaniel Dett, Carl Ditton, and John Rosamond Johnson's musical compositions paved the way for other African American musicians. Bunk Johnson, Ferdinand "Jelly Roll" Morton, Meade Lux Lewis, Art Tatum, Thomas "Fats" Waller, Louis Armstrong, Duke Ellington, and Earl "Fatha" Hines laid the foundation for jazz—America's original art form.

Hattie McDaniel was the first black person to win an Academy Award. She was named the Best Supporting Actress for her role as Mammy in Gone With the Wind (1939). Since then, Academy Awards have been won by three other black performers: Sidney Poitier (actor), Whoopi Goldberg (supporting actress), and Denzel Washington (supporting actor). Canada Lee (Leonard C. Canagata) was a leading theater and film actor during the 1940s and 1950s.

Mary McLeod Bethune established a school for black children in Daytona Beach, Florida. She was president of Bethune-Cookman College for twenty-five years and adviser to four U.S. presidents, beginning with Herbert Hoover in 1930. Booker T. Washington, born into slavery, acquired an education after Emancipation and went on to be the principal of the Tuskegee Institute in Alabama from 1881 to 1915, during which time the Institute became a national leader in industrial and vocational education. George Washington Carver, a botanist and chemist, was born a slave. After earning a master's degree at

Iowa State Agricultural College in 1889, he was appointed head of Tuskegee Institute's Department of Agriculture. One of our most honored scientists, Carver developed over three hundred uses for peanuts and sweet potatoes. Charles S. Johnson, E. Franklin Frazier, and Ira De A. Reid were renowned sociologists. W. Allison Davis achieved honors in childhood education, and Abraham Harris was a successful economist.

The list of famous black authors is even more impressive. Gwendolyn Brooks won the 1950 Pulitzer Prize for poetry; Toni Morrison won the 1993 Nobel Prize in literature. Prominent early black writers include Paul Laurence Dunbar, Countee Cullen, Langston Hughes, Mari E. Evans, Leroi Jones (Amari Baraka), Sterling Brown, Zora Neale Hurston, and James Weldon Johnson. Numerous black American fiction writers have set high standards of excellence: Richard Wright, Frank Yerby, Jessie Fauset, Jean Toomer, James Baldwin, and Claude McKay. Lorraine Hansberry was an award-winning playwright. Her most famous work, *Raisin in the Sun*, was also made into a movie.

The formal literature of social protest written by Frederick Douglass, Samuel Ringold Williams, and W. E. B. Du Bois has been cited by social activists throughout the world. Du Bois was the author of the first monograph in the Harvard Historical Series, and he wrote the first autobiographical study of the African American community. George Williams, author of *History of the Negro Race in America*, and Carter G. Woodson, founder of the *Journal of Negro History*, became the first renowned African American historians.

Ralph Bunche was awarded the Nobel Peace Prize in 1950 for successfully mediating an end to the Arab-Israeli conflict caused when Israel was founded. Martin Luther King Jr. received it in 1964. In the field of law, Thurgood Marshall was the first black to serve as a U.S. Supreme Court justice. He was appointed in 1967 by President Lyndon Johnson.

Black American pioneers in professional sports include Bill Pickett, star of rodeos; basketball players Charles Cooper Jr. of the Boston Celtics and Nat Sweetwater Clifton of the New York Knickerbockers; baseball player Jackie Robinson of the Brooklyn Dodgers; football players Fritz Pollard of the Akron Indians, Joe Lillard of the Chicago Cardinals, Kenny Washington and Woody Strode of the Los Angeles Rams, and Bill Willis and Marion Motley of the Cleveland Browns; boxing champions Jack Johnson and Joe Louis; golfers Charlie Sifford, the Long Beach Open champion in 1957, and Tiger Woods, Masters Tournament (1997) champion; and the 1875 (first) Kentucky Derby winner, Oliver Lewis. Althea Gibson was the Wimbledon tennis champion in 1957 and U.S. champion in 1958. Arthur Ashe was the Wimbledon tennis champion in 1975. Of special mention is Henry Armstrong, the first and only fighter to hold three titles at once: featherweight, lightweight, and welterweight.

Numerous schools are accelerating their efforts to teach black history, to help black students learn about their cultural heritage. In some schools, for example, black heritage is taught as an integral part of regular school subjects. In such schools Crispus Attucks is becoming as well known as Paul Revere, and the works of black writers like Langston Hughes, James Baldwin, Gwendolyn Brooks, and Ralph Ellison stand beside those of Charles Dickens, Jane Austen, and Jack London. Even bulletin board displays and school musicals and plays are taking on a black look. Black students are getting acquainted with nineteenth-century black intellectuals such as Edward Blyden, Martin Delaney, and David Walker. Furthermore, they are learning to respect the revolutionary ideals of early black abolitionists and twentieth-century civil rights leaders such as Martin Luther King Jr., Malcolm X, Whitney Young Jr., Roy Wilkins, Shirley Chisholm, and Medgar Evers. The subtle message of this educational journey for black children is this: welcome to blackness, you too are America.

Noteworthy abolitionists crossed the color line. Many white colonists condemned slavery and fought against it, often in the face of great danger. The first formal protest to reach a legislative body was made by the Quakers of Germantown, Pennsylvania, in 1688 and renewed in 1693 and 1696. These protests ignited a debate that spread throughout the colonies. A few brave slaves also joined in public protest by asking for their freedom from bondage, and a large number of free blacks demanded that colonial legislatures put an end to slavery. In 1764 James Otis wrote the pamphlet, "Rights of the British Colonies," in which he declared that blacks had an inalienable right to freedom (Franklin 1988). Theologians, including Samuel Hopkins of Rhode Island, Ezra Stiles of Connecticut, and Jeremy Belknap of Massachusetts, publicly advocated the abolition of slavery.

Quaker minister John Woolman epitomized the individual efforts of white colonists to abolish slavery. Beginning in 1743, he traveled throughout the South, the middle colonies, and New England, encouraging slaveholders to accept the necessity of manumission (freeing) of slaves. His 1754 publication, *Some Considerations on the Keeping of Negroes*, was the first public proclamation by a religious body condemning slavery. Prominent leaders in the fight for colonial independence, including Benjamin Franklin and Benjamin Rush, also agitated for the abolition of slavery, as did influential lawyers like Zepheniah Swift, Noah Webster, and Theodore Dwight. In 1785 John Jay became president of the newly formed New York Society for Promoting the Manumission of Slaves. Other founding fathers who spoke out against slavery were John Adams, Albert Gallatin, Alexander Hamilton, George Washington, Patrick Henry, and Thomas Jefferson. In fact, in the first draft of the Declaration of Independence, Jefferson took George III to task for not abolishing the slave trade. But Southern representatives in the Continental Congress were able to get the language stricken from the final document. (Recent scholarship, unfortunately, indicates that Jefferson's antislavery sentiments were questionable.)

There were many vocal black abolitionists in the 1800s. In 1829 David Walker, a free black, wrote *Appeal*, wherein he described the oppressive conditions of slavery, encouraged all blacks to seek the best education available to them, chided white Christians for allowing slavery to exist, and encouraged slaves to rebel. Georgia offered a $10,000 reward for the capture of Walker. The best-known black abolitionist, however, was Frederick Douglass. Born a slave in 1817, he escaped to New York in 1838. His best-selling book *Narrative* recounted his life. Douglass established a newspaper, the *North Star*, in which his poignant editorials stirred countless readers to condemn slavery.

The most notorious white abolitionist in the 1800s was William Lloyd Garrison, editor of an antislavery newspaper, the *Liberator*, established in 1831. Garrison's antislavery editorials incited an attack by a white mob in Boston in 1835. Other well-known white abolitionists included Theodore Weld, author of the book *Slavery As It Is*; Horace Greeley, editor of an antislavery newspaper, the *New York Tribune*; writers Ralph Waldo Emerson, Julia Ward Howe, Harriet Beecher Stowe, Henry Wadsworth Longfellow, Lydia M. Child, Walt Whitman, and John Greenleaf Whittier. Occasionally there were defectors, pseudoliberators who abandoned the abolition cause. An 1863 saying by free blacks captured the black American sentiment about those persons: "Save us from our friends—we know, understand, and can cope with our enemies. We know them; we have them under control."

Barely Holding On

How tragic it is that, after more than four hundred years, few white Americans know black history, that many whites become upset when a day, a week, or a month is set aside to celebrate black history. Equally important, many blacks themselves know little about that history, having been deprived of learning about it in an educational system that ignored them, both past and present. "Why is it," a pensive black college student asked a white professor, "that most white Americans know more about civilizations and peoples that lived thousands of years ago in places thousands of miles away than they know about black people very much alive who live only a few blocks or a few miles away?"

"It's a matter of priority," the professor answered.

"Next time there's a war, I won't fight for this country," the student vowed. "That will be a matter of priority too."

Without the opportunity to learn about their past and (especially for low-income blacks) without hope that the white educational system and white-dominated world of work will offer any solutions for them, many African Americans have become disenfranchised. There is no single response to being black *and* the descendant of slaves; some individuals withdraw, others clown, many assume proud mannerisms, and others become aggressive and turn to crime. Numerous black males like James Baldwin (1964) observed,

> The boys, it was clear, would rise no higher than their fathers. School began to reveal itself, therefore, as a child's game that one could not win, and boys dropped out of school.... I no longer had any illusions about what an education could do for me; I had already encountered too many college-graduate handymen (31).

Many black youth have seen no opportunities other than crime:

> Crime became real, for example—for the first time—not as a possibility but the possibility [for being a way to survive]. One would never improve one's circumstances by working and saving one's pennies, and besides, the social treatment accorded even the most successful [blacks] proved that one needed, in order

to be free, something more than a bank account (33-34).

Whatever the pattern of response, most low-income blacks have been tempted to reject and disavow all that is American. Yet it is not the American dream that is repulsive to them but their inability to participate in it.

Turning once more to Langston Hughes, we can see the frustration black Americans feel:

What happens to a dream deferred?
Does it dry up
Like a raisin in the sun?
Or fester like a sore—
And then run?
Does it stink like rotten meat?
Or crust and sugar over—
Like a syrupy sweet?
Maybe it just sags
Like a heavy load.
Or does it explode?

—"Dream Deferred"
Langston Hughes

Chapter 3

Talking Black, Thinking Black: Communication and Values

Many African Americans are bicultural and bilingual. They are able to think and speak in ways that are functional for survival in both white and black cultures. For example, they may think in standard (white) English and speak standard English. Thinking white/talking white is most common among black Americans who are integrated into mainstream society. These blacks who talk white and think white are frequently criticized as being conformists and are, not surprisingly, the easiest individuals for whites to deal with because they adhere to the dominant white social norms and talk in a way whites can understand. What they communicate to whites who will listen is, "I'm not like those other [black] people. I'm like you."

Most acculturated blacks, however, talk white while thinking black. That is, even though they act very much like white Americans, they also maintain beliefs, behaviors, and ways of seeing the world that characterize tradition-oriented blacks. Thinking black and speaking standard English also allows blacks to at least control their interpretation of embarrassing or volatile racial situations, thereby saving face or forestalling harm. This is common during black-white conflict. It is a way to *git ovah on* (deceive or fool) white people.

Thinking black and talking black is the third way blacks communicate in interracial situations. It usually occurs for two reasons: (1) blacks have not become fluent in standard English or (2) they are fluent in standard English but completely frustrated and have decided to express their feelings in what for them is "true" speech. Richard, a black factory worker, illustrates this type of situation.

> Ain't no telling what white folks will do. My boss accused me of copping Zs [sleeping] on the job. He jacked [humiliated] me in front of the brothers [black workers]. It don't take all that to talk to me. I went left on him [lost my composure] and told him, "Yeah, I was tore up [drunk], but I thought we be tight [friends] and you'd cut me some slack. That was my bad [mistake]. We ain't tight, but I can get off on this job [perform well].

Richard lost his job because his supervisor, Jim, misunderstood him and concluded that he was incorrigible. If Jim had asked Richard in a private conversation to state clearly, in standard English, why he was sleeping on the job, a reprimand might have salvaged a potentially good worker. Later, Jim verbalized his discomfort with Richard when he compared him with Paul, a black carpenter who also worked for Jim and who talked white: "Paul don't talk black like Richard. He talks like me."

Communication Behaviors

Thinking and talking black/white is part of a larger issue: basic communication patterns between black and white Americans. For a better understanding of this issue, let us consider in greater detail similarities and differences between African American and European American communication styles. People who speak different languages live in different worlds. This is true even among people who speak the same language (more or less) and share geographical (but not cultural) boundaries, as do white Americans and black Americans. They are in the same environment, but not the same culture.

It is important to note here that we will be discussing generalized communication patterns and the reader must remember that well-founded generalizations, while helpful, will not allow one to understand individuals in an ethnic group who deviate from that group's patterns of interacting. Such generalizations provide only a reliable starting point. Also, basic processes of relationship building such as being sensitive to social courtesies transcend black-white interactions. All people prefer that outsiders respect them and try to understand their cultural values (Hall 1976; Henderson, 1989).

Culture-based communication styles are illustrated in ways other than just speech. Nonverbal communication also reflects a group's culture. Tradition-oriented black Americans, for example, may walk away from authority figures after being reprimanded in a way that communicates disgust with the reprimand. The passively hostile person may smile and say, "Yes, sir," or "Yes, ma'am," but his or her movements or inflection may say just the opposite. An arrogant swagger nonverbally communicates defiance, indicating, in black English vernacular, "Bump that" or "It don't take all that."

Conditioned by their childhood socialization process of continuous flirtation with the forbidden and testing of boundaries, black adults interact with friends and strangers using behavior that friends consider appropriate and strangers, particularly whites, often consider brusque or hostile. This challenging of authority is usually done without malice; however, to uninformed white Americans, especially managers and supervisors, this behavior is often seen as disconcerting, if not disrespectful. Vague or indecisive whites in the workplace are seldom successful in setting limits for blacks without creating conflict. Lucy, a black salesclerk, thinking black and talking black, had such an encounter with her white supervisor.

We had this big staff meeting to decide how to increase sales. The sup [supervisor] said to me, "You

don't follow all the company procedures." And I
copped a plea [disagreed], "Why you getting off [pick-
ing] on me? What you want me to do?" Like a silly
ninny, she answered, "What can you do to improve
your sales? What do you suggest?" When I said, "I'll
just keep on keeping on [doing what I been doing],"
she got mad. If she didn't have a plan, she shouldn't
call a meeting. We need a business meeting not a sensitivity session. That "what do you want to do" stuff
don't cut it with me.

The supervisor should have been specific and told Lucy
what procedures she was not following and the consequences for not following them. More specific to the reason for the meeting, she should have, as Lucy suggested,
had a plan. And within the plan, she should clearly delin-
eate appropriate staff behavior. Lucy was not being an
obstructionist when she asked: "What do you want me to
do?" The supervisor should have told her.

Blacks and whites tend to approach disagreements differently. In a heated debate, for example, whites are likely
to want to immediately defuse the situation by shutting
down the discussion ("I don't want to talk about this now.
You're too emotional!"), but blacks prefer emotion to
avoidance, which they view as being hypocritical, devious, or insincere. The black discussion style is confronta-
tional, personal, and loud; whites prefer nonconfronta-
tional, impersonal, and quiet discussions. Thus, whites tend
to see blacks as contentious, argumentative, and threatening. Within these contexts, blacks put the search for truth
before peace, whereas whites put peace before truth
(Kochman 1981).

Uninformed observers may also misinterpret the
nonverbals of blacks in a heated discussion. One person
may turn his back to the group, take a step or two without saying anything, and return to the discussion to make
yet another point. This is seldom a sign of disagreement.
The movement itself *is* the point. It is a nonverbal way of

saying "I agree" or, in black English, "Right on" or "I'm down with that."

In most white cultures anyone may start a conversation. However, once a conversation is initiated, it is impolite to interrupt the speaker. Turn taking, which is regulated by pauses in the conversation and vocal cues that indicate the speaker is finished, is the norm. The listener encourages the speaker to continue talking by nodding his or her head, smiling, or raising the eyebrows. Similar to white Americans, anyone can start a conversation in black American culture. However, it is generally accepted that the listener can interrupt the speaker with brief rejoinders to correct untrue statements. These corrections tend to be brief (e.g., "I didn't say (do) that," "That's a lie"), and once the correction is made, turn taking continues. Unlike white Americans, black Americans sometimes "call out" their request for additional information with comments such as "And what else?" "Speak," "Tell it like it is"—a carryover from the traditional church behavior noted in chapter 1.

Eurocentric white people tend to look intently (stare) at each other while they are talking. To most white Americans, eye contact indicates attentiveness, respect, and confidence. The eyes, a popular saying goes, are the window of the soul. Thus, white Americans are taught to look into the eyes of people with whom they are conversing, though the speaker will look away occasionally to avoid staring. If the listener looks away, however, it may be interpreted as disrespect, disinterest, a lack of confidence, or dishonesty. A tradition-oriented black American tends to look at an individual when addressing remarks to him or her but to periodically look away when the other person is talking. This is especially true if the other person is older or occupies a position of authority. To stare at high-status people while they are speaking is a sign of disrespect, of not giving that person his or her "propers" (respect). Giving someone "the evil eye" is an ultimate expression of disapproval. The evil eye is a cold, glaring stare, and if blacks give higher-status whites the evil eye, they are most often completely frustrated or in a state of rage.

If the eyes are the window of the soul for white Americans, then the face mirrors the emotional feelings seen in the window. That is, facial expressions are vital clues to white Americans' feelings about a topic or a behavior. A smile, for example, usually means happiness and a frown, unhappiness. However, many white Americans are taught, "If you can't say something nice, don't say anything at all." Thus, they learn to mask emotions, and when this happens, a smile is a "false face." Facial expressions of African Americans are similar to those of European Americans, though unpleasant feelings are more likely to be masked when blacks interact with white people.

Black humor, particularly as addressed to whites, often masks disappointment, anger, and sometimes self-debasement. Most whites hear joviality in the black jester's humor; a few perceptive individuals hear the sorrow. Langston Hughes's poem "The Jester" invites such empathy:

> In one hand
> I hold tragedy
> And in the other
> Comedy,—
> Masks for the soul.
> Laugh with me.
> You would laugh!
> Weep with me.
> You would weep!
> Tears are my laughter.
> Laughter is my pain.
> Cry at my grinning mouth
> If you will.
> Laugh at my sorrow's reign.

—"The Jester"
Langston Hughes

The ease with which some blacks joke about adversity—losing a job, being passed over for a promotion, and so forth—is often mistaken by whites as being a sign of lack of initiative, incompetence, apathy, or some similar inadequacy.

> White Supervisor: Hey Joe? Come here for a minute.
> Joe: Sir?
> Supervisor: I'm afraid I've got bad news for you.
> Joe: Sir?
> Supervisor: I'm going to have to let you go.
> Joe, grinning: Hell, boss, don't feel bad. Now I can sleep as late as I want to. [He laughs and does a brief dance.]
> Outside the plant, Joe rams his right fist into the rear of his car and cries, but he had gone out as a man; he hadn't let the supervisor see his fear of being unemployed.

Black humor, Langston Hughes (1966) wrote, is laughing at what you do not have when you know you should have it; or at what you wish were not funny but it is. Whites who laugh at black humor often miss the emotional profundity of the situation. They fail to understand its serious import. In many ways, black humor is inexpensive therapy. Of course, the price to be paid for burying anger or disappointment within oneself is a high degree of stress, and black males in particular usually pay it. Stress-induced illnesses are leading causes of death among black Americans.

While speaking, most whites are less animated than blacks and therefore have difficulty capturing the attention of black audiences. Generally, white Americans avoid being excessively loud. When they converse in educational and business settings, they speak with little modulation of pitch and disapprove of loud, nasal tones or strident voices. (There is considerably more vocal variety when white people talk with friends in informal settings.) Blacks use a lot of hand gestures when they talk. Indeed, black speakers frequently put their entire body into a speech, waving their hands and gesticulating at every juncture. The volume and pitch of their speech increase as their interest in the topic increases. Loud conversation, similar to loud music, signifies exuberance. Emotional speakers are likely to be judged by blacks as self-assured and sincere. Unemotional speakers are likely to be seen as phony or insincere.

In every culture there are special forms of words, or types of conversation, which are thought to be appropriate for the particular situation. White Americans, for example, prefer directness and value openness, while black Americans regard openness as a form of weakness or treachery and try to prevent whites from penetrating their thoughts. White Americans' direct verbal style reflects their true intentions, which embody their needs and desires in the interaction process. Black Americans' indirect verbal style, in contrast, consists of verbal messages that camouflage and conceal their true intentions, which embody *their* needs and desires. As noted in chapter 1, the traditional black American family is ideally suited to reinforcing this kind of behavior because it teaches its members ways to express themselves and at the same time minimize being punished by whites. This then is the process of preparing family members to survive in the larger society but not at the cost of being nonexpressive. For instance, angry blacks learn how to "tell off" whites in a way that leaves the blacks with a feeling of dignity but which is indirect enough so that whites misread the message.

> Richard, a black engineer, had just been publicly upbraided for an error in his project design. On his way out of the staff meeting, Kenneth, his supervisor, asked him to come to his office. Once they were in his office, Kenneth asked Richard, "Do you have any problems with me chewing you out about the design error?"
>
> "Why didn't you tell me here instead of in front of the other guys?" Richard asked.

"I want them to know that if they mess up, I'll get on them too," Kenneth explained.

"How's your wife?" Richard asked.

Kenneth raised his eyebrows in surprise. "She's okay," he said.

"Give her my best." Richard smiled as he thought: My worst lovemaking is better than your best.

Trying to get back to the original issue, Kenneth, slightly flushed, asked, "Are you alright with my criticism?"

"Are you?" Richard smiled.

In the span of a few minutes, he had told Kenneth that he was upset with being publicly criticized and he was also able to play a little game of the "dozens" with his unsuspecting supervisor. Next time, he thought as he left the office, I'll ask about his mama.

The issue of "giving face," especially to people with high status, is important to black Americans. They take great care not to embarrass people publicly. This does not mean, however, that rude or hateful people are entitled to be given face. They are publicly rebuked for violating the norm. Black people who are rude to others are told to "cool it" or risk having "the black beat off you." It is wrong to "talk smack," that is, to address someone in a disrespectful manner.

There is also great variance in black and white cultures regarding the use of silence. Euro-Americans tend to be very talkative and to become uncomfortable with protracted silence. While generally talkative, blacks are not uncomfortable with silence. An idea from Zen Buddhism, also found in African folklore, has influenced African cultures in this attitude toward silence: "He who knows does not speak and he who speaks does not know." African Americans learn early on to listen not only to what is said but also to what is *not* said. Sometimes the most important part of a message is not spoken. People of traditional black cultures want all the facts about a situation before rendering an opinion. They will ask probing questions:

"What else did he say?" "Then what did she do?" "What did you say?" "What did you do?" Moreover, they are hesitant to "meddle," especially when mutual friends are involved in a conflict.

Values Contrasts

Black American values can be examined within the framework of five aspects of culture: (1) the nature of reality and truth, (2) the nature of time, (3) the nature of space, (4) the relationship of humans to nature, and (5) the nature of human relationships.* It may be surprising for white Americans to learn that African Americans share the same or similar values and behaviors with American Indians and peoples from Third-World countries in Africa, Latin America, and parts of Asia. As we examine the value orientations listed above, the common characteristics will become apparent.

Reality and Truth

Every culture has a set of shared assumptions about the meaning of reality and how one determines what is real. Most white cultures tend to define reality empirically by applying objective rational analysis and the scientific method. Non-Western cultures, particularly Third-World cultures, American Indians, and African Americans, determine reality subjectively. Tradition-oriented black Americans make no clear distinction between mind and body—spirits can influence human events, and social reality can be understood out of context; meanings may vary, categories of things may change, and causality is ambiguous. For most white Americans, events cannot be understood out of context; meanings do not vary, categories of things do not change, and causality is not ambiguous. The following exchange between a white supervisor and a black mechanic illustrates this point:

---

* Adapted from Florence R. Kluckhohn and Fred L. Strodtbeck, *Variations in Value Orientations.* Evanson, IL: Row, Peterson, 1961.

Supervisor: Good morning, Mr. Sampson.
Chief Mechanic: Good morning, ma'am.
Supervisor: Are you in charge of the maintenance on this airplane?
Chief Mechanic: Yes, ma'am.
Supervisor (smiling): Great. What step are you at on the checklist?
Chief Mechanic: I'm...I'm not sure.
Supervisor: Oh? Haven't you been told to follow the checklist? Don't you understand that if you follow the checklist, there will be no problems?
Chief Mechanic: Well, ma'am, I don't want to be disrespectful but each plane is unique. I know how to follow a checklist, but each airplane is different. I have the best feel for what's wrong with this airplane. Besides, equipment and me are like one [All you white folks think about is rules].
Supervisor (visibly irritated): The only thing you have to feel are the pages of that checklist. Why is it so difficult for you to do something as simple as read the directions and follow them? You'll get the job done faster and more efficiently [And cut out that "equipment and me" crap].
Chief Mechanic: I follow what the engines tell me when I listen to them. Some things shouldn't be rushed [Let me do this my way].
Supervisor: Well, you better start listening to what I tell you.
Chief Mechanic: But.... (He picks up the checklist and begins work on the airplane.) Yes, ma'am, I'm doing the steps now.

The supervisor would have been better received if she had focused on the reasons it was important for Sampson to follow the steps in the manual. After her explanation, she could have asked, "Does that make sense to you?" If he answered, "No," she could have asked him to explain what didn't. Better yet, she could have given Sampson "face" by noting their differences in perspective, asking him how planes are unique and what he hears when he listens to them. "You and I seem to have different ways to get the job done. Perhaps there is something I'm not aware of. Please tell me more about the differences among airplanes." In other words, she should have kept an open mind. If Sampson had made suggestions that might have improved the work process, she could have routed them through administrative channels for review and possible implementation. Of course, if his reasoning was faulty, she could have insisted that he carry out her original directive.

Evil spirits are another part of black cultural reality not often shared by whites. Thus, a white supervisor is likely to have difficulty accepting as sincere the statement of a black subordinate who believes that the quality of his work is deteriorating because a neighbor put a hex on him. Conversely, the subordinate will not be responsive to his supervisor's admonishment, "Evil spells aren't real and they can't affect your work." A more helpful approach would be for the supervisor to ask, "What can I do to help you minimize the hex while you are on the job so that your productivity will improve?" Often the answer is, "There's nothing you can do except to understand that I'm under stress and trying to deal with it." In this instance, an appropriate reply would be, "Let me know if the stress becomes too much for you so we can find a way for you to do your job." The supervisor, while not buying into a belief in evil spirits, has demonstrated respect for the employee's genuine distress and concentrated on trying to help him improve his productivity on the job.

Time

Cultural assumptions determine how time is defined, measured, and valued, thereby determining whether an individual is "late," "early," or "on time" and whether someone has "wasted time" or has enough time. In modern societies, just as in ancient ones, the concept of time imposes a structure on work and leisure. Most white Americans are *monochronic*—they compartmentalize activities and do only one thing at a time. They are linear in thinking, sequential in behavior, clock-oriented, and work-oriented. One of their most valued possessions is their appointment calendar. Tradition-oriented black Americans (those who "think black") are *polychronic*. "Colored people's time" means not being driven by the need to keep rigid time schedules. They do many things at the same time, are circular in behavior and repetitive in speech, and believe that time is not of the essence. When black employees with this orientation toward time are driven by monochronic job requirements, they often do poorly and receive low performance ratings. The following incident illustrates this point:

Paul, a white supervisor, waits for Mary, a black cashier, to come to work. She is late again. Fifteen minutes after her shift is supposed to begin, Mary arrives in a rush.

Paul: You're late again! Why are you late?

Mary: (Avoiding Paul's glare, she punches her time card.)

Paul: (He motions for Mary to follow him into his office.) Now, explain something to me. Why were you late again?

Mary: Well, this morning I got tied up in traffic.

Paul: This morning? What about yesterday, and the day before? What about the day before that?

Mary: I think yesterday I had trouble deciding what to wear, and once I got that straightened out I had to iron my clothes. I also had trouble getting my hair right. Oh, and the day before that my alarm clock didn't work.

Paul: So more than one thing keeps you from getting here on time?

Mary: Yes....

Paul: I've told you a dozen times that you're expected to be here on time. Don't you understand that?

Mary: What do you mean?

Paul: I mean that you punch a clock like everyone else—and you're expected to punch it on time.

Mary: But I do get here as soon as I can.

Paul: Can't you get up earlier?

Mary: I get up early. I've got other things to do in the morning besides just getting to work.

Paul: Can't someone else do those things?

Mary: No one else can fix my hair.

Paul: Have you thought about how your being late is affecting the other cashiers? Especially those on the earlier shift? They would like to get home on time.

Mary: Yes, I know. But sometimes I'm early and whoever I relieve gets to go early. I think it washes out even in the end. Nobody's ever complained to me. Has Brenda complained to you?

Paul: Whether someone complained or not isn't the point. The point is that I need you here on time. The other cashiers get here on time. You figure out a way to do it, or else....

Mary: Don't I do good work? Nobody's ever complained about my work.

Paul: You're not listening to me. Next time you're late and don't have an acceptable reason, I'll fire you.

The supervisor could have handled the situation more empathetically and been more effective. Mary was a good worker, so he could have said something like this: "Mary, you're one of my best cashiers. But your tardiness is not acceptable. Perhaps we can come up with something that will satisfy you and me. The only thing I cannot negotiate is your starting time. Whatever shift you work, you must start on time. What can you do to get to work on time? And what can I do to help you?"

Space

How people use space is culturally determined and is an integral aspect of power and of interracial relationships, having both physical and social meanings. Social and personal distance are an important part of the way cultures deal with space. In the United States there are four kinds of "normal distance"—intimate, personal, social, and public—within which there are "very near" and "very far" comfort zones. Black Americans and white Americans consider intimate contact and touching as being "very near." Most white Americans consider a space of eighteen to thirty inches near enough for personal distance, even for conversations in crowded places. When this space is lessened, they back away so as not to be too close. Black Americans, on the other hand, stand closer during personal conversations. Most prefer to "get in your face" when discussing important issues, especially if the conversation is positive. Some blacks gently slap each other's right hand (giving skin) when an important point is being made. More so than whites, blacks give high fives or low fives as gestures of agreement. Angry blacks, however, will move toward or away from other persons, depending on whether they believe they can change the other person's opinions through closer dialogue or whether the situation is too volatile and more space might prevent an escalation of disagreement.

Social distance during formal activities, which is greater than in personal conversations, allows an individual to talk to several people at once. Here, too, black Americans stand closer than white Americans, whose comfort zone is four to seven feet. During public activities such as banquets and keynote speeches, distances of twelve to twenty-five feet are considered near for both white and black Americans; beyond twenty-five feet is far.

White employees generally desire more privacy than black employees. Arrangement of work space can provide for these variances. Black people in the workplace tend to become extended family members within their work units or departments. Therefore, as described in chapter 1, close interaction and cooperation are important. Physical barriers impede the interaction and often disrupt the work flow. In essence, tradition-oriented blacks work better in open-door or open-space environments than they do in closed-door, closed-space work settings.

Paul Barnett, vice president in charge of sales, heeded his CEO's directive to "shape this place up and do whatever you can to make it look less like a social club and more like a sales department." Paul commissioned an office systems consultant to redesign the office to include a receptionist area, a large conference room, and individual offices that had floor-to-ceiling partitions. After the design was approved by the CEO, Paul asked the four sales representatives to choose their offices. Mary and Denice, black salespersons, requested the conference room. Sarah and Richard, white salespersons, gleefully selected private offices. When told that they could not have the conference room, Mary and Denice asked if they could have the partition that separated their offices removed.

"Out of the question," Paul insisted. "This new arrangement will give both of you more privacy and the means to work more efficiently."

Denice winked at Mary. "Well, girlfriend, I guess you'll have to bring your own lunch and talk to yourself." They both laughed.

"What's so funny?" Paul asked angrily.

"Nothing's funny," Denice frowned. "I'm dead serious. We're a team, Mary and me. We answer each other's phones, share client information, and, if we could, we'd share clothes."

Puzzled by Mary and Denice's reluctance to select offices, Paul abruptly ended the meeting. "I expect all of you to move into your offices and get on with your jobs."

Six weeks later, Paul read the quarterly sales report. Sarah and Richard's sales had increased 8 percent, while Mary and Denice's sales had declined 10 percent.

If Paul had been more sensitive to his employees' spatial preferences, he could have accomplished his goal of making the office look more professional and also not alienated Denice and Mary by involving all of the sales staff in creating a new design. Having floor-to-ceiling walls might not have been as important to Sarah and Richard as having more privacy, which could have been in the form of partial walls between work spaces. Thus, instead of removing a wall as requested by Mary and Denice, a partial wall would have given them the feeling of being consulted. It also would have allowed them to freely communicate with each other.

There are negative consequences to both whites and blacks when interacting with two different sets of spatial comfort requirements. When their zones, or territory, are invaded or they in turn invade the territory of others, whites tend to communicate their discomfort or apologize for the intrusion. Blacks tend to remain silent. Because the physical comfort zone is closer for blacks than it is for whites, some whites are literally pushed around the room during conversations with blacks who move into the white individual's discomfort zone. In the office where Denice and Mary worked, the walls were important for maintaining Sarah's and Richard's privacy and spatial comfort zones, but they had the opposite effect on Denice and Mary.

What was at work here, of course, was a difference between blacks and whites in how they use space and what their privacy needs are. Blacks are more inclined to share the space they work and live in, and they don't have the privacy needs of whites, who consider intrusions on their privacy a serious breach of social etiquette—if not a violation of the law!

Relationship to Nature

The relationship between nature and humans in Western cultures is radically different from that in most Third-World cultures. Tradition-oriented black Americans, like many from these cultures, perceive humans as a part of nature, with which they must be in harmony because they are eternally inseparable. Thus, black Americans try to adapt to their natural surroundings rather than dominate them.

White Americans tend to see humans as "subjects" whose "object" is nature, which they have the right to confront, exploit, and dominate. Consequently, they are frequently at war with nature. This resolute and sometimes reckless drive to control the physical world is diametrically opposed to the adaptive attitude of black Americans.

Abdul Anderson, a black executive, sat quietly and listened to the proposal for the remote recycling plant. This is going to be a fine plant, he thought. After Bill Jones, a white architect, finished his presentation, Abdul asked, "Aren't there any trees on the plant grounds?"

"Yes, sir," Bill grinned proudly, pointing to the small trees in the drawing. "We'll have several."

"But these are young trees. It looks like they are from a nursery," Abdul observed.

"Yes, they will be strategically planted to complement the architectural ambiance," he bragged.

Abdul frowned and stared at a picture of the existing plot. "What about the trees that are there?" he asked, pointing to an area in the northeast corner.

"They will be cut down. It's more cost-effective to cut them down than to design a building to incorporate them," Bill responded.

"How expensive?" Abdul asked.

"About $100,000 or more, sir," Bill sighed.

"How long do you think it will take our new trees to look like these?" Abdul pointed to a close-up photograph of the trees that would be cut down.

Bill thought for a few minutes, scratched his head, and said, "About fifty years."

"We'll never have the pleasure of such beauty, will we, Bill?" Abdul mulled.

"No sir, but we'll have the pleasure of not being over budget with this project," Bill smiled.

"Too bad," Abdul said as he reluctantly approved the plan.

For a few minutes, Bill thought Abdul would make the foolish decision of causing the design to be altered to save the trees. For a few minutes, Abdul thought he had the courage to do the right thing and save the old trees.

Human Relationships

In individualistic cultures people are taught to take care of themselves and their immediate families; in collectivist cultures people belong to groups or collectivities that look after them in exchange for loyalty. White American culture is generally considered one of the world's most individualistic cultures. Having a weak or no permanent base in family and friends, each individual's orientation toward life and the environment is self-reliance; that is to say, white Americans are conditioned to think for themselves, to make their own decisions, and to carve out their own futures by their own initiative. This is embodied in the ideal of "self-actualization" and an "I" identity. Black American culture is group-oriented, characterized by interdependence, a "we" identity, and interpersonal ties that permanently unite family and friends. In the workplace, white Americans don't expect, or even want, a close or dependent relationship with a supervisor. Black managers and executives, on the other hand, tend to form friendships and mentor-mentoree relationships that are stable and supportive. Failure to understand the differences in expectations regarding a mentoring relationship is illustrated in the following interaction between Mike, an African American, and his white supervisor.

Here is what happened during the first interview between Mike and his supervisor relative to the nature and value of the mentoring procedure and its potential impact on Mike's career:

Supervisor: Mike, come on in. Good to see you (slaps him on the back). Have a seat.

Mike: Thank you, sir.

Supervisor: How are you doing? Everything going okay for you in the research department? I hear you have some new folks over there.

Mike: Yes, it's going great. New people, new assignment.

Supervisor: Well, let's discuss this mentoring program that you're in. I believe it's the best in the industry, and I support it wholeheartedly. We've been doing this for three years, and I've been involved since the beginning. I've seen many bright men and women walk through our doors and become top salespeople and managers. Do you know Ron Zabel, Ida Mikowsky, and Tyrone Zimmerman? I've sponsored them, and they're in the midmanagement program now, and Ida is due for a promotion any day.

Mike: Wow, that's great! I know them all, they're friends of mine. Ida showed me where the cafeteria was, Ron set up my computer for me, and Tyrone gave me all of his old files.

Supervisor: Well, the same opportunities and successes the others have achieved are also within your reach. I'm proud of the successes I've had as a mentor. I'm sure you'll make it in this company. I'm here to help and offer advice—just let me know how I can help you.

Mike: I'm really excited and I want to succeed. I'm glad that you're in my corner. I can't lose!

Supervisor: You'll do fine, Mike. I have full confidence in you. Good luck!

Here is what happened at the performance feedback session some time later:

Supervisor: Mike, come in and have a seat.

Mike: Thanks. Sorry I'm late but I was with our buddy, Tyrone. He was showing me the new campaign for product development.

Supervisor: I've got a meeting at 10:30 so I'll make this brief. I asked you to meet with me to discuss your final performance review for the mentoring program.

Mike: Yeah, I heard how some other guys in the research department got promoted to marketing. I can't wait.

Supervisor: I've got bad news, Mike. You did not graduate from the program. You failed the basic marketing tests, you didn't enroll in the required correspondence courses, and you've been late on your draft proposals to me.

Mike: You're joking, right?

Supervisor: No, I'm not.

Mike: What? I can't believe this! You said you'd take care of me. You said that I'd ace the program just like Tyrone and the others (points his finger and jumps out of his chair). You lied! And those draft proposals—that's a joke. I can do the real stuff, I don't need to work on drafts. And you said get them to you when I could. You didn't say exactly when you wanted them. I can't believe that you won't help me.

Supervisor: Mike, I said I had full confidence in your abilities to complete the program, not my ability to take care of you. I know my abilities and have proven myself. I thought you understood the seriousness and intensity of this program. Everything you needed to do was outlined in the mentorship handbook, which was given to you and explained at the orientation—and you signed the contract. I told you to come to me if and when you needed help. I can't help you now—it's too late.

Mike and his supervisor had very different expectations for the mentoring program. Mike expected his supervisor to voluntarily tell him everything he needed to do to succeed. His supervisor expected Mike to get his guidance from the handbook and to ask him for any help he needed. In Mike's culture, friends tell each other "like it is." One does not have to ask for information or guidance. It is common for Mike's friends to approach each other and volunteer helpful information. In Mike's perception the supervisor should have gone over the details of the mentor program guidelines with him, set specific time lines for getting things done, and periodically checked to see how Mike was getting along.

Effective Communication

With practice and determination, most white Americans can learn to communicate effectively with black Americans. In order to do this, they must focus their mental energies on listening and gear their behavior toward producing a *positive response*. This means learning to sustain one's attention while listening by eliminating cultural filters and barriers that prevent reception of the complete message.

First, white speakers must try to rid themselves of the false belief that communicating with African Americans is only a matter of hearing them. Communication across cultures is more than hearing—it is *using words with the same meanings that they have for blacks*. Listening does not occur in the ears; it takes place between the ears. Communication occurs only when the person who sends a message and the person who receives it have the same picture in their minds. Whites and blacks regularly misinterpret each other's messages. Much of this is because some individuals hear only what they want to hear. If Joclyn (a black woman) says, for example, "This place is cold [unfriendly]," her white colleague, Marilyn, may misread the statement to mean "This place needs more heat." A sensitive response would be to ask Joclyn whether she is talking about the temperature or the social atmosphere. Asking for clarification or rephrasing what the other person said and checking its accuracy are ways to minimize misunderstandings.

General appearance, attitude, mannerisms, and language and speech characteristics can all contribute to (or detract from) effective communication. Let's look at each of them.

General Appearance

Whites who communicate effectively with blacks discount the size, weight, complexion, dress, and posture of blacks with whom they are speaking. When confronted with physically unattractive black individuals, they say to themselves, "This person may have something important to say. His (her) appearance sends a negative message to me, but he (she) is trying to tell me something that is more important than physical appearance. I am going to try to find out what it is." Unfortunately, by focusing on how blacks look instead of what they say, whites who want to understand blacks frequently miss the moment (as do blacks in responding to whites).

Attitude

Savvy white people tell themselves that if a black speaker is flippant, overbearing, argumentative, or arrogant, these characteristics are ingrained and difficult to change. Further, they tell themselves, "This person's attitude does not affect what he (she) has to say. It only colors how it is said. I shall do everything I can to separate his (her) ideas from the negative first impression I have gotten." Some individuals suffer from a self-righteousness that prevents them from recognizing their own negative attitude.

Mannerisms

White Americans who want to communicate effectively with blacks are not discouraged or threatened by blacks who behave in a "hip" or "cool" way. These things do not affect the real value of what a black person has to offer. Thoughtful whites say to themselves, "These mannerisms have little or no relationship to what the person is saying. They are cultural behaviors, and I will try not to let myself be influenced by them." More often than not the mannerisms are part of an emotional toughness blacks believe is necessary to cope with racism.

Language and Speech Characteristics

Effective white communicators do not ridicule black people who speak with an accent or a dialect. Admittedly, they are sometimes difficult to understand, but this is not a

valid reason to routinely tune them out. Whites who successfully communicate with blacks say to themselves, "This
will not be easy, but I am going to try extra hard to understand this person. I may have to ask for clarification fairly
often, but I won't ask the person to speak 'correctly.'"
The inviolability of a black American's personhood is so
important that some resist any assault, no matter how
minor, on their ways of communicating.

Establishing Cross-Cultural Relationships

The above aspects, while important, don't go far enough.
Guidelines are needed for whites to establish successful
working relationships with blacks. Carl R. Rogers (1958)
succinctly described a process for effectively establishing
relationships across cultures. That process, embodied here
in five questions, suits our purpose well.

> *Can I be perceived by the other person as trustwor-*
> *thy, as dependable in some deep sense?* (12)

This is more than being rigidly consistent. It means being able to keep appointments, fulfill promises, and not
abandon the relationship when conflict occurs. Black
Americans value friendship with white people who, as one
man stated, "are there through thick and thin." Some
blacks will intentionally initiate conflict, such as calling
whites racists, to see how willing they are to pursue a friendship. It is important that white Americans do not send
double messages; their words and behavior must be consonant. "My word is my bond" is not just rhetoric among
blacks. Whites and blacks must do what they promise or
have an acceptable reason for not doing so.

> *Can I be expressive enough as a person that what I*
> *am will be communicated unambiguously?* (12)

If whites are unaware of their own feelings about black
Americans, a double message of acceptance-rejection will
be sent. Therefore, it is important for whites to clearly
communicate to blacks regarding their beliefs, values, and
intentions. "What you see is what you get" must take on

true meaning. Most Americans are as concerned about what people do not stand for as what they do.

Can I let myself experience positive attitudes toward this other person—attitudes of warmth, caring, liking, interest, respect? (12)

An attitude of aloofness or superiority is unlikely to lead to lasting relationships with blacks. Such attitudes create social barriers that wall off blacks and whites from each other. Impersonal business interactions can sometimes succeed under these conditions, but not personal relationships.

Can I receive him as he is? Can I communicate this attitude? Or can I only receive him conditionally, acceptant of some aspects of his feelings and silently or openly disapproving of other aspects? (13-14)

Whites are usually threatened by aspects of blacks' appearance or behavior, for example, black English or different clothing styles. "I don't want them [white coworkers] to wear my clothes," a black female factory worker complained to her foreman. "I only want them to respect my right to dress as I want—just as I accept their styles."

Can I step in his private world so completely that I lose all desire to evaluate or judge it? Can I enter it so sensitively that I can move about in it freely without trampling on meanings which are precious to him? Can I sense it so accurately that I can catch not only the meanings of his experience which are obvious to him, but those meanings which are only implicit, which he sees dimly or as confusion? (14)

No white person can feel like a black person (or vice versa), but each may be able to understand, be sensitive to, and respect the other. Even though each black American is shaped by his or her racial group, white Americans must remember that each black person is a unique individual. When confronted by blacks who are culturally different, effective whites don't try to create the illusion that all blacks are alike, which fosters stereotyping, ignores individual uniqueness, and may cause destructive identity conflict.

Levels of Communication

In his book *Why Am I Afraid to Tell You Who I Am?*
John Powell (1969) concluded that few people who are
involved in friendships want to be inauthentic, but the fears
and risks involved in honest communication seem so great
and so volatile that most people hide their real feelings.
This is unfortunate, because the most rancorous problems
between blacks and whites revolve around inauthentic
communication, that is, not sharing themselves authenti-
cally with each other. Countless individuals can testify to
the fact that sharing one's feelings has the potential to open
minds, to give individuals a new awareness of people who
are culturally different. Powell's five levels of communication describe this process.

The outer, or fifth, level of communication is the "cliché
conversation." Everyone remains at a safe emotional distance; there is no sharing of deep personal thoughts. Conversations are superficial, such as "Hello." "Hello. How
are you?" "Fine, thank you." "I'll be seeing you." "So
long." The other person senses the superficiality and obliges
by giving polite answers. This is the kind of communication that most often takes place between blacks and whites,
even among many persons who claim to be "close friends."
The comfort level of both parties remains intact.

The fourth level is the "reporting of facts about others." At this level the participants give the erroneous appearance of sharing intimate things about themselves. Instead of talking about themselves, however, they tell others what so-and-so has done or said; they seek emotional
shelter in gossip or trivia, but they volunteer nothing about
themselves. At this level, blacks and whites get to know
each other as passionless persons. Thus, blacks and whites
discover only a few pieces of the other persons' personalities. Similar to level five, this is a relatively safe kind of
place for interracial interaction. It is also a barren place
for constructive change.

At the third level of interracial communication, "ideas and judgments," the relationship becomes slightly more authentic. But caution more than honesty is the guiding rule. That is, the participants watch one another closely and retreat if the other persons narrow their eyes or show some other form of disapproval. Even worse, they resort to saying things they do not mean because they imagine that is what the other individuals want to hear. At this level we might hear such things as "I agree with you" or "That's a good approach," when actually the speaker neither agrees nor believes the approach is good. This method of "going along" with someone in order to "get along" with him or her is also a common form of black-white communication.

The second level, "feelings and emotions," is characterized by openness and honesty. This requires raw courage, but without this kind of communication, black-white relations will not grow. By stating their true feelings, blacks and whites establish authentic relationships. To tell someone truthfully "I am angry with you," "I am happy with you," "I am frightened of you," or "I am jealous of you" exemplifies the gargantuan step in race relations that blacks and whites must take together in order to be friends. When this happens, feelings of alienation, apathy, anguish, and cynicism are shared and understood. So too are feelings of inclusion, interest, joy, and hope. Then and only then are blacks and whites able to sincerely get along with each other—the first level.

Talk Is Cheap, Action Expensive

When communicating with each other about racially sensitive topics, whites and blacks should choose their words carefully. Inappropriate or unexplained words can cause the initial encounter to be the final encounter, as in the conversation below.

Black Male Client: I'm embarrassed to talk about
being treated like an animal.... This situation is dif-

ficult for me. [Maybe she will spare me further em-
barrassment and tell me what to do.]

   White Female Social Worker: Are you telling me
it is painful for you to talk about this? [He will see
that I am empathetic.]

   Black Client: Yeah, that's right. [Hell, didn't she
hear me? Why is she rubbing my nose in it?]

   Social Worker: What do you mean by "embar-
rassment" and "difficult"? Can you tell me what you
feel when you say those words? What are you feeling now?

   Client: (Silent, he stares at the floor.) [I knew it
was a mistake to come here.]

   Social Worker: We all have difficulty describing
certain feelings. It's okay. I want to help you. [He's
really getting into this. I can help him.]

   Client: Maybe I didn't make myself clear.... I need
time to think about this. [This was a mistake. I don't
need to be psychologized. I need to get out of here.]

   Social Worker: We can do this next week. Maybe
next week you will feel like talking about your feelings. [I'll have to go slower with him.]

The client did not return to the agency. To him, the social worker was nothing more than a busybody. She did
not appear to have any immediate help for him. She did
not err by paraphrasing the client's remarks. Her mistake
was to not cast her restatements within the context of the
services she provided (e.g., "Are you telling me it is painful for you to talk about this because you don't know how
it might be used by me to help you?" or "Are you embarrassed to talk about this because I might use the information to hurt you?"). The last thing he needed was "to be
psychologized."

Black Americans often complain among themselves
about white people "playing mind games" with them—
using jargon or fancy words, probing sensitive issues, and
otherwise embarrassing them. "They [white people]
shouldn't bring fire [disturbance] if they can't stand being

burned [hurt]," a black waiter concluded after losing his job for hitting a white customer who was "messin" with him. In fact, the customer thought he had given the man a compliment: "I've been listening to you, and you never have a dangling participle." The waiter interpreted the remark as: "You ain't got no balls." Interestingly, from the white perspective, blacks who use black English may be perceived as using jargon, probing sensitive issues, and otherwise embarrassing whites, too. The most effective common ground is built on both parties using as clearly as possible the vocabulary they are most comfortable with, whether it is standard English or black English or a mixture of the two. In the above incident, while the white customer was probably not trying to insult the black waiter, it is likely that he was being patronizing.

Altercations that involve race issues cause many well-meaning white Americans to overreact. And their consternation increases if the blacks they are interacting with are belligerent. In such instances, asking blacks what is bothering them provides for blacks an opportunity to get some things out into the open. The negative perception some whites have of combative blacks, particularly individuals whom they must help, is a barrier to maximizing the value of the encounter. But, as illustrated in the following case, the barrier may be surmountable:

> African American Female Client: I have to tell you up front, Mr. Cooper, I think you and your white friends are the main reasons my people are in bad shape. You sit in your sterile office, listening to elevator music and deciding if I'm going to get the things I need. Now, just tell me what you want from me. (She looks out the window.)

> White American Male Social Worker: I'll do all that I can to help you, Mrs. Adams. I hope that you don't let my race, my choice of music, clothes, food, or anything else come between us. My job is to see that you get adequate housing. Have I done anything to offend you?

Client: (She glares at the social worker.) My, my, ain't we the good white people!

Social Worker: Here are the forms. I need you to complete them and return them to me as soon as possible. If you wish, Mrs. Adams, we can go over them together before you leave so that I can answer your questions.

Client: More middle-class white bullshit paperwork. You people are going to kill me with paper. I can read. I don't need you to read these to me.

The social worker maintained a calm, nondefensive manner. By keeping his cool, he avoided giving the woman an excuse to be even more hostile. He did not take on the client's caustic remarks about him or white people. Instead, he gave her the forms and focused on the helping process—not her ethnicity or their social class differences or her animosity. He patiently worked with her and got her placed in an acceptable apartment. Consequently, the social worker proved his empathy through *behavior*, not talk. During their last conference, she was able to acknowledge the social worker's efforts and her confrontive demeanor.

Social Worker: I'm glad that you and the children like the apartment, Mrs. Adams. Is there anything else I can do for you?

Client: You've been a gem, Mr. Cooper. I wasn't very nice to you, was I? I owe you an apology for my behavior during those first meetings.

Social Worker: Your behavior probably seemed appropriate to you at the time. A lot of things had happened to you to cause that behavior. Besides, you didn't know me. You were reacting to what you thought I represented. I'm glad that you see me differently now. You don't really owe me an apology— but I accept it. I hope if you need help again, Mrs. Adams, that you'll turn to me.

Mrs. Adams's change in demeanor is surprising or seems phony only if we believe that, unlike whites, blacks are incapable of contrition.

The willingness of blacks to continue interacting with white agency personnel is affected in part by the attractiveness of the arrangement (what is in it for them?) and in part by the belief that only through a cooperative effort can they achieve certain goals. It is not enough to encourage blacks to have an open discussion; whites must be able to help them in some way. The recommended course of action is anything that will help black Americans to survive and thrive. As a young black worker said to his white supervisor, "Talk is cheap. Action can be expensive."

Allowing open, honest expression of feelings obviates the need to hide anger. Candid expression of feelings to whites will probably be a new experience for many blacks. White people seldom ask them what they think; they usually tell them what they should think. Thus, as will be discussed in succeeding chapters, when asked to participate in open-ended discussions, most blacks will be unprepared and even hesitant to do so. Empathetic whites may still be hesitant to attempt to communicate with blacks because of the risk of exposing themselves to black anger and aggression. They may also fear being "put down" or ridiculed by "smart" blacks, having their prejudices exposed, being verbally abused, or even changing their own negative opinions about blacks.

These risks are great, but the rewards are even greater for those who take them, which if done in the right spirit, can be a major leap forward. Friendships with blacks often grow out of the honest expression of feelings followed by positive interactions. And these friendships tend to be lifelong and exemplary.

The following tips extrapolated and recast from advice E. Paul Torrance (1970) gave teachers may, to a significant degree, help reduce the risk for whites who want to establish a meaningful dialogue with blacks.
1. *"Wanting to know."* This occurs when whites ask blacks questions, become absorbed in the search for truth about black-white similarities and differences, and try to make sense out of this knowledge.

2. *"Digging deeper."* Truly caring persons are not satisfied with quick, easy, superficial answers about black
people. They know that not all blacks are neatly positioned on the "black side" of the race relations divide.
Some of them are on the "white side"; others are im-
paled on the wall—wavering between both sides. One
must look carefully to find the truth.

3. *"Looking twice."* The helpful white person is never
satisfied with learning about blacks only from a distance. He or she will want to get to know some of
them from different angles and perspectives; that is, to
get to know some of them personally.

4. *"Listening to a cat."* Too many people can neither talk
nor listen with understanding to a cat. That is just
another way of saying that many people have difficulty dealing with nonverbal communication. Words
are insufficient in communicating one's deepest and
most genuine concerns to other people. White Americans and black Americans must be able to interpret
each other's nonverbal behavior if they want to relate
to each other at deeper levels.

5. *"Crossing out mistakes."* Whites who try to help blacks
inevitably make mistakes. But they refuse to avoid the
encounter because of the fear of failure. Blacks also
must be able to cross out their mistakes with productive behavior.

6. *"Getting into and out of deep water."* Testing the limits of one's race-relations knowledge and skills requires
taking calculated risks. It also requires asking blacks
questions for which sometimes ready answers do not
exist.

7. *"Cutting a hole to see through."* By opening up the
windows of their own minds and being open to new
things, whites can see blacks more clearly and be better seen by them.

8. *"Building sand castles."* In order to build a sand castle one must be able to see sand not only as it is but also as it might become. In race relations, this means being able to start from an existing situation and, based on a strategy of change, alter it or create a new one.

9. *"Singing in their own key."* Thoreau stated this idea very poetically: "If a man does not keep pace with his companions, perhaps it is because he hears a different drummer. Let him step to the music he hears, however measured or far away. It is not important that he matures as an apple tree or an oak. Shall he turn his spring into summer...?" Whites can facilitate positive relations with blacks by letting them tell their story in their own way. In that way, blacks can best communicate objective facts and subjective interpretations of them.

Part II

Community, School, and Workplace

Chapter 4

Black Communities and the Perils of Segregation

The problems of dependent families, neglected and maladjusted children, the aged, the sick and disabled, the unemployed and underemployed, as well as the search for social identity and status, occur among all ethnic groups in the United States, European Americans included. These problems are, however, accentuated in black communities. The prerequisites for a constructive and successful life—conforming to amorphous "white" standards—are constantly increasing and becoming more complex, and growing numbers of low-income black Americans are falling through the cracks, becoming an underclass. Having little success competing for educational and employment opportunities, they consequently fade into the landscape and become "shadow people"—nameless, faceless individuals whose plight is often misunderstood, forgotten, or ignored. These people find it devastating to be have-nots in a society that has so much wealth. Failure to understand the different social classes in black America, particularly the poor and the underclass, is tantamount to not understanding blacks or the reasons for their rage.

Black Class Differences

The black community is more complex and perhaps more divided than white Americans might imagine. Middle-class,

working-class, and underclass blacks are not an amalgam-
ated, undifferentiated whole. Income, education, and hope
(or hopelessness) divide the black community as surely as
color unites it. All black Americans try desperately to
maintain a sense of worth and dignity, yet only a small
percentage of middle-class blacks and fewer still of poor
and underclass blacks achieve the recognition they desire.

Middle Class

More than 80 percent of black middle-class families live
in husband-wife households. These families are among
some of America's most remarkable success stories. Fifty
years ago the term *black middle class* largely meant people
who worked as waiters, porters, barbers, and similar low-
status occupations. Today it refers to teachers, lawyers,
dentists, engineers, and business executives. Their children
usually graduate from high school, and many of them attend college or vocational and technical schools (R. M.
Clark 1984; Evans 1993). Middle-class blacks enjoy all
the benefits of the civil rights revolution—better education, more money, more access to power, and more acco-
lades than any previous generation of African Americans.
Even so, according to a 1995 Kaiser Family Foundation/
Harvard University poll, most of the black middle-class
respondents said they were victims of overt racial discrimination.

Middle-class black Americans are also subject to income
discrimination. As a group they earn less than middle-class
whites. In 1996 the black per capita income was only 56
percent of white income. The median income of black families was $26,500; for white families it was $47,100. Furthermore, middle-class blacks possess less actual wealth.
For example, in 1996 blacks possessed ten cents for every
dollar of wealth held by middle-class whites and only 5
percent of black families owned stocks or pension funds,
compared with 25 percent of white families that had them.
Factors that cause these disparities include skewed access

to jobs and limited access to home mortgages. It has been well documented that home ownership is the single most important means of acquiring other assets, yet housing discrimination has cost the current generation of middle-class black Americans $82 billion (Jackman and Jackman 1980; Oliver and Shapiro 1995).

Even with the racial and income disparities, however, the black middle class is the gold standard of socioeconomic mobility in black communities. Middle-class blacks are black "society." They give credence to the civil rights slogan "If you can conceive it, you can achieve it." Indeed, many middle-class blacks not only think upscale, they live upscale in expensive residences, wear designer clothes, take exotic vacations, and belong to exclusive clubs.

The black middle class is the vanguard that inches its way into previously white domains—neighborhoods, schools, and jobs. For blacks who cannot escape or do not want to leave black communities, they provide a myriad of businesses, social organizations, and community services, including restaurants, theaters, banks, insurance companies, newspapers, magazines, barbershops, beauty shops, churches, fraternities, sororities, and civic clubs. Modern middle-class blacks are black America's dream of upward mobility come true. Lower-class blacks are waiting impatiently to join their ranks, and each year that they wait brings a wider division between the two classes.

Little has changed since E. Franklin Frazier wrote *Black Bourgeoisie* (1957), a seminal book about the black middle class. Similar to middle-class white Americans, they foster the norm of self-reliance. Unlike middle-class white Americans, however, their self-reliance is group-centered, not individual. For them, survival of the race is more important than survival of the individual. Consequently, because they value their ethnicity and group identity, middle-class blacks have provided most of the leadership during twentieth-century civil rights movements. In contrast, lower-class black Americans generally value their race but not at the peril of their individual survival. This makes even more miraculous the civil rights activities in the 1960s that put thousands of lower-class blacks in harm's way when they publicly protested racial segregation and discrimination. Indeed, lower-class blacks were the civilian corps civil rights leaders mobilized for boycotts, sit-ins, stand-ins, pray-ins, and mass meetings throughout the South.

From the perspective of the family, middle-class blacks place more importance on family unity and mutal support than they do on the needs of individual family members. Poor blacks, on the other hand, are more ready to risk the disintegration of the family if their financial or emotional needs are severe enough.

Middle-class black women carry the major burden of holding the family together, though, of course, they have other problems as well. One poignant issue for them lies in color discrimination and the competition they experience from white women.

Trellie Jeffers, quoted in Alice Walker's (1983) book *In Search of Our Mothers' Gardens*, condemns the black middle class for neglecting black (dark-skinned) black women:

> The black middle class has for generations excluded the black black woman from the mainstream of black middle-class society, and it has, by its discrimination against her, induced in itself a divisive cancer that has chopped the black race in this country into polarized sections; consequently the black middle class has devoured its own soul and is doomed, a large number of working class people believe, to extinction (294-95).

Intragroup discrimination crosses racial lines when middle-class black women sometimes find themselves competing with white women for jobs and the companionship of black men. The 1997 Million Woman March in Philadelphia called national attention to the fact that not only are white women more likely to have higher incomes than black women, they are also more attractive to some black men. When it is talked about in middle-class social circles, it rarely comes out as eloquently as it does in Gwendolyn Brooks's (1972) words: "Black women must remember, through all the prattle about walking or not walking three or twelve steps behind or ahead of 'her' male, that her personhood precedes her femalehood; that sweet as sex may be, she cannot endlessly brood on Black Man's blonds..." (204). But they do brood. And sometimes they brood in the presence of white women, who are seen as unnecessary competitors.

Serving as gatekeepers of various community opportunities, middle-class blacks seldom choose to serve as mentors to upwardly mobile working-class blacks. As a result, poorer residents find the black community to be a place of contradictions. They are encouraged on the one hand to display initiative and tenacity in working for the good of the community, while on the other, they must passively submit to black middle-class authority. They are called upon to be more involved in community projects but are often chided in public for being too aggressive. They are urged to publicly support black community leaders but discouraged from privately challenging them. They are able to conform with a minimum of discomfort. It is cruel irony that low-status blacks have a long history of being an oppressed minority group and of obeying others' demands.

As the education and income gaps increase between middle-class and lower-class blacks, the derisive words lower-class blacks use to describe uppity middle-class blacks also increase: *Afro-Saxon; European Negro; Ann* (a black woman who acts "white"); *Aunt Jane* and *Aunt Thomasina* (a black woman who does not support black civil rights initiatives); *house nigga* (a black who makes excuses for whites and white racism); *token* (a black person placed in a job or position because of pressure from blacks, but who seldom promotes black causes); and *Tom* and *Uncle Tom* (a black man who betrays other blacks).

Lower Class

Black American children born into low-income families begin life facing higher odds against survival than white children (J. Jones 1993; Slaughter 1988). They are more likely to die in infancy than white babies. If a black baby lives, the chances of losing his or her mother in childbirth are four times higher than for the white baby. The black baby is usually born into a family that lives in the inner city, a family that tends to be larger than its white counterpart and crowded into dilapidated housing that is structurally unsound or unable to keep out cold, rain, snow, rats, and insects. The average birth rate for low-income black families is over 150 percent greater than that for the nation as a whole. With more mouths to feed, more babies to clothe, and more needs to satisfy, the average black family is forced to exist on a median family income that is barely half the median white family income. Almost half of America's black children under the age of six live in poverty as compared with less than 15 percent of white children. The local school often offers no avenue to a well-paying job, much less to fame or fortune.

To be poor and black too often means social isolation from middle-class people—white and black—who through ignorance, insensitivity, or malice address poor blacks in offensive ways, calling them "culturally deprived" or even "retarded." Labeling of this kind is bound to be humiliating, and it may cause those labeled to be unduly hostile toward otherwise well-meaning whites and blacks. Further distancing occurs when middle-class whites refer to lower- and middle-class blacks as "you people." This sets up "us-them" relationships in which neither lower- nor middle-class blacks are part of "us"—and lower-class blacks are not even part of the middle-class black "us."

Lower-class black families can be divided into two groups. First is the family that lacks substantial material possessions but whose members receive enough warmth and emotional support to assure relatively normal social development. The second type of family lacks both material objects and emotional support; parents may be indifferent to their children's needs, largely through ignorance. With proper care, members of this kind of family can make satisfactory social adjustments.

Contrary to public perception, most of the black lower class are not recipients of welfare (U.S. Bureau of the Census 1992). Typical lower-class black parents have less than a tenth-grade education and are employed as unskilled or service workers, their family income often less than the minimum wage. They do not get their names in the news as outstanding representatives of their race or ethnic group, but neither do they show up in crime statistics. Their children usually manage to keep out of trouble, and they are not what might generally be thought of as "uneducable." Yet these children are likely to be overlooked when teachers want someone to pose for a picture or to represent the school in some special way. They frequently do not qualify for school programs designed to help the poor and disadvantaged because their parents earn a few dollars more than program guidelines specify.

Not all children from lower-class black families—welfare or nonwelfare—enter school with a readiness to fail, but failure is often inevitable. These children are in a narrowly constructed social class box—built for them by society—from which they can seldom escape. Behaving as any trapped person would, many of these children become hostile toward adults who constantly demand a higher degree of restraint and self-control than they themselves exhibit; hostile toward teachers who force-feed them unwanted facts, assignments, and rules; and hostile toward themselves for being born. Many parents sense these feelings and try unsuccessfully to help their children escape. In the end, school personnel and insensitive human services personnel slowly shut the box, leaving the children trapped inside.

Families that give their children the best preparation for succeeding in school tend to have the following:

- *Family conversation that* answers children's questions and encourages them to ask questions; extends their vocabulary with verbs, adjectives, and adverbs; and empowers them to explain their points of view and to stand up for them;

- A *family environment that* encourages and participates in reading; provides a variety of toys and play materials with various colors, sizes, and objects that challenge children's imagination and creativity;

- *Two parents* who read, read to their children, value education, and reward their children for school achievement.

More often than not, poor black children will not have this kind of preparation because they are members of very large families; thus, their parents do not have the time to give each child needed positive reinforcement. In contrast, middle-class black children come from smaller families; they are usually given tasks to perform and rewarded for successful completion.

Parent-child verbal interaction in many lower-class black homes is limited to commands. Some parents try to protect their children by telling them what to do, but very few actually have the time or energy to discuss problems. Home is a world of "no" and "hush," and these children soon develop the ability to tune out these commands. Parents seldom read to their children, and problem-solving toys are luxuries which the budget does not include.

Black neighborhoods may be the only place where economically disadvantaged black people can find friendship, acceptance, and recognition. But they usually do not. *Recognition* and *status* in the community are monopolized by middle-class blacks. Thus, while middle-class blacks feel the burden of discrimination by whites, the lower-income and underclass blacks are oppressed by whites and often by middle-class blacks as well. *Even community social activi-*

ties often take a form that for low-status poor blacks is actually antisocial, for example, neighborhood school dances where purchasing tickets is prohibitive for most low-income youths or at school social functions, where black parents tend to feel unwanted. Feeling confused and powerless, some lower-class black Americans learn not to learn, learn not to see, learn not to hear insults. They are mastering the art of psychologically dropping out of society.

The degree of powerlessness experienced by lower-income black adults also detracts significantly from their ability to be concerned with their children's social development. Most lower-class black adults work, unfortunately at jobs that pay low wages. To be unemployed or underemployed in black communities is a continuing condition. Few new jobs are added to replace the low-paying, inner-city employment being phased out by advanced technology. Feeling trapped in an impersonal system, low-income black adults pass on their feelings of powerlessness to their children. Some black adults give their children an additional legacy: resignation and defeat.

Of course, in some affluent homes parents also neglect their children's development. Often the major difference between lower- and middle-class black homes is not the degree of parental interaction with children but instead the number of *parent substitutes* who are available to the children. Affluent black parents can afford baby-sitters, tutors, camps, and psychiatrists to care for their children. In most inner-city communities there are few parent substitutes. For a variety of reasons, then, lower-class black families do not adequately prepare their children for school.

Most lower-class black children, unlike middle-class black children, must learn how to learn school-related functions after they enter school and will probably not be prepared for the rewards and punishments or the standards of success that characterize public schools. Research suggests that the social deficits are so great for some black children that they never catch up with their white agemates (R. M. Clark 1984).

Therefore, it is difficult for teachers to convince these children that school is a good place and worthy of their best efforts. This does not mean that all parents of low-achieving black students are hostile or indifferent toward the school; most of them hope that somehow their children will achieve success there. Indeed, education is perceived by most lower-class black parents as their children's only way out of poverty. Rather than being against education, they are hesitant to become involved with it. Few black children who grow up in lower-class homes want to be silent spectators, yet culture and custom require them to be quiet. Most of these children do not cry out against the inhumanity they suffer. Zora Neale Hurston (1942) was such a child:

> One of the most serious objections to me was that having nothing, I still did not know how to be humble. A child in my place ought to realize I was lucky to have a roof over my head and anything to eat at all. And from their point of view, they were right. From mine, my stomach pains were the least of my sufferings. I could not reveal myself for lack of expression, and then for lack of hope of understanding, even if I could have found the words. I was not comfortable to have around (117).

The Underclass

If middle-class and lower-class black Americans are difficult for white Americans to understand, poverty-stricken black Americans, the underclass, are an enigma to all. Lately, they have become frequent subjects of research and of welfare experiments. Yet, despite the attention directed at them, they seem to become even more disadvantaged. The economic and social gains achieved by middle-income and affluent blacks have little meaning for poverty-stricken blacks. Housing, employment, and educational opportunities are primarily for middle-income blacks and a few fortunate low-income blacks. Even the so-called antipoverty programs do a better job employing middle-class black administrators than finding jobs for black welfare recipients. Before white social services personnel and educators can interact successfully with poverty-stricken black Americans, they must be aware of the physical and social environments of underclass communities and know something about the homes of the poorest of the poor and, above all, what it takes to survive in a subculture of poverty.

The underclass family is composed largely of individuals whose family life is characterized by filth, inadequate diet, and extreme alienation. These people tend to be psychologically and organically fragile, easily bruised or broken. They are truly culturally different from middle-class people. This family type constitutes a small minority of black families, but it is what many whites believe is the majority.

Caught up in a cycle of poverty and neglect, these people are preoccupied with the immediate needs of survival—getting adequate food, housing, clothing, and medical care. Whether they live in urban or rural communities, life for members of the black underclass is the quintessence of economic and racial oppression. Barbara Jordan wrote, "Although we have had the courage to deplore it, we have failed to heal the gap between the middle-class black…and the black slum dweller, who hates us almost as much as he hates Whitey" (Haskins 1977, 79). Or as Marian Wright Edelman (1988) observed, all of the expensive cars and clothes cannot hide the black middle class from poverty-stricken blacks. Affluent blacks must take care, as Langston Hughes wrote in the poem "Snob," not to distance themselves from the black lower class and underclass.

    If your reputation
    In the community is good
    Don't snub the other fellow—
    It might be misunderstood—
    Because a good reputation
    Can commit suicide

By holding its head
Too far to one side.

—"Snob"
Langston Hughes

Whites also need to guard against writing off the underclass and assuming that poor black mothers give their children no moral guidance. An old proverb states that poverty does not destroy virtue, nor wealth bestow it. John Hope Franklin and Eleanor Holmes Norton (1989) offered this rebuttal to white Americans who believe that most black Americans, especially those in the inner city, lack strong, positive family values:

> Blacks have always embraced the central values of [American] society, augmented those values in response to the unique experiences of slavery and subordination, incorporated them into a strong religious tradition, and espoused them fervently and persistently. These values—among them, the primacy of family, the importance of education, and the necessity for individual enterprise and hard work—have been matched by a strong set of civic values, ironic in the face of racial discrimination—espousal of the rights and responsibilities of freedom, commitment to country, and adherence to the democratic creed (3-4).

Most poor black parents are intensely aware of their poverty and easily embarrassed by it; too many white Americans respond to them in patronizing and humiliating ways.

Physical Environment

Physical appearance is one of the most revealing characteristics of the poverty-stricken urban neighborhood; neglect and disorder are common. Buildings are in a state of deterioration, highlighting structural neglect and social decline: "There is something about poverty that smells like death. Dead dreams dropping off the heart like leaves in a dry season and rotting around the feet; impulses smother too long in the fetid air of underground caves" (Hurston 1942, 116). Slum neighborhoods are overcrowded with buildings, and the buildings are overcrowded with people. Their inhabitants consist mainly of those who are not welcome or cannot afford to live elsewhere. Slums have poor sanitation, and the garbage-strewn streets and alleys are overrun by rats. Infant and maternal mortality rates are high; so too are unemployment and underemployment. Vice is rampant. Slums are the habitat of occupationally marginal men and women and the hiding place of fugitives. For most residents, it is easier to get drugs than it is to get a job. Norman Jordan reminds us of that horrible fact:

I have seen them trying....
to sober up
to be heard
to listen
to live—
Lord knows, I have seen them.

I have seen them waiting....
for relief
for a job
for winter to pass
for life—
Yes Lord, I have seen them.

I have seen them crying....
because it's too late
because they can't feed their babies
because they are tired of maybe
because they are afraid—

dear Lord yes, I have seen them
Praying...
for miracles.

—"I Have Seen Them"
Norman Jordan
in *Complete Poems*

This kind of community can be thought of as a place of anonymity and alienation. Except for families that do not have the means to leave, the people are transient, moving from one rundown neighborhood to another. They often do not know or trust their neighbors. The children of these communities (if they can be labeled as such) often show the physical signs of their hard lives—they age more quickly than affluent blacks. Socially, they become little old "men" and "women" before reaching chronological maturity. This condition is compounded by the fact that these children are but the continuation of generations of hopelessness.

Many studies have documented the ill-health of underclass children. Suffering from malnutrition, physical defects, and social and physical neglect, they are like children in the poor, Third-World countries. The inability of most inner-city residents to secure adequate physical and psychological health care condemns them to the role of breeders of the poor.

Home and School Environments

Given such surroundings, it is easy to see the origins of some of the problems poverty-stricken urban residents face. Recreational facilities are almost nonexistent, and children play in the streets and alleys. Parents who are fortunate enough to get jobs must work long hours to earn barely enough for subsistence. When they get home, these parents are often so tired or worried about where the next meal will come from or how they are going to earn next month's rent that they don't have energy left to pay attention to their children. This is not to say that the children are unloved, but that they often *feel* unloved. Frustration-tolerance levels are low among these poverty-stricken parents, who tend to discipline their children with a "good whipping." At the same time, parents tend to exercise little jurisdiction over preschool children, who come and go as they please. Older siblings become mamas and papas for the younger ones. There are rarely books in the home, and even if books are available, the lighting may be too poor for children to read—if they know how to read.

Home experiences are either the beginning or the curtailment of a child's readiness for formal middle-class-oriented educational experiences, but underclass black students are generally not given the preparation at home that will allow them to succeed in school. While middle- and upper-class black children generally view school as being an extension of the home, poor black children usually view school as an environment separate from and often antagonistic to the home. To the underclass black child, home is home and school is school and it is difficult for educators to bridge the two.

Some poverty-stricken parents are not concerned about inferior schools. They believe that it is more important for their children to quit school and get a job. Thus, many black children are forced to leave school and get a job as soon as they can legally do so; others must work after school to help their families.

Male Identity Crisis

As noted earlier, lower- and underclass black families tend to be mother-dominated, a circumstance that can be traced back to slavery. Hundreds of years of economic, social, and psychological brutalization have emasculated the black male to the extent that he has seldom been the stabilizing force in his family. Historically, it has been difficult for black men to obtain work, whereas it has always been easy for black women to secure menial jobs. Many poverty-stricken black males see life as a never-ending struggle to free themselves from the domination of women (Aldridge 1991) but often become casualties of self–inflicted wounds in the process.

The black American male's resentment of female domination may be exhibited in various behavior patterns such as sleeping all day and staying out all night, drinking, or beating his wife and children. Often the underclass adult male finds his home life unbearable and leaves, sometimes never returning, sometimes returning only when the welfare checks arrive. Viewing this human tragedy, which is reenacted in each successive generation, the black male child responds by being aggressive or, worse, apathetic. Black males know only too well that they must find their manhood or suffer total psychological emasculation. Many black males respond by setting up their own rules and becoming their own authorities. Low-income black adolescent males in particular try to assert their masculinity when publicly challenged by whites.

The Importance of Housing

With considerable insight, Toni Cade Bambara (1974) said that home is where most black people share their "next-to-nothing things and their more-than-hoped for wealth" (76). This same sense of family caused Barbara Jordan to reminisce, "We were all black and we were all poor and we were all right there in place. For us, the larger community didn't exist" (Haskins 1977, 8). Whatever their socioeconomic situation, home for most black Americans is where the hope for a better life originates. Bill Cosby talked about role models for black children at the graduation speech he gave at Morehouse College in Atlanta, Georgia, on February 10, 1985: "If you want to see a positive image, it's in your house. It's standing there washing your underwear. If you want to see a positive image, it's cooking your dinner and has a job to go to in the morning."

Melvin L. Oliver and Thomas M. Shapiro (1995) describe housing as an important aspect of wealth that goes beyond the significance of income per se. Wealth is what people own; income is what they receive from work, social welfare, or retirement funds. The extent to which housing leads to wealth is an accurate indicator of individual and family opportunities to secure a good life in whatever form they desire—education, health, business, justice, and so on. Each year Americans are given two highly publicized lists: (1) the year's highest income earners and (2) the nation's wealthiest citizens. The first list includes many African Americans, mainly athletes, performing artists, and entertainers. The second list, published by *Forbes* magazine, profiles individuals whose assets or command over monetary resources place them at the top of the American economic hierarchy. Few black Americans appear on the *Forbes* list, and their absence is no accident.

Racial differences in wealth are the consequences of differences in social class, access to human capital (education, jobs, etc.), propensity to save money, consumption patterns, and racial discrimination. The bottom line is that historically, compared with whites, blacks have not had equal opportunities to amass wealth, especially through the ownership of property.

Historical Overview

Black slaves were denied the opportunity to acquire land, build communities, and otherwise accumulate wealth. After the Emancipation Proclamation, local, state, and federal laws greatly limited blacks' access to decent housing, high-wage employment, and business ownership. During the Reconstruction era, Southern blacks were purportedly allowed to acquire land through the Southern Homestead Act of 1866. However, the legislation that was meant to provide confiscated plantation land to former slaves was amended to include Southern whites who swore that they had not taken up arms against the Union or given comfort to the Confederates. Consequently, over 75 percent of the land applicants were white. Further restricting their opportunities to acquire and develop land, blacks were often charged illegal homestead fees and given the worst land (Lanza 1990). Almost no blacks became wealthy as a result of this act.

Discrimination in housing and land ownership created disparate socioeconomic opportunities for white and black Americans. Throughout the nineteenth century, a sizable number of white families who secured title to land were able to finance a good education for their children, provide resources for their own or their children's upward mobility, and secure rights through political activities. America was indeed a place in which white citizens and immigrants could realize their dreams for success. Most blacks realized only their nightmares.

In the early twentieth century, the federal government launched its first national initiative to increase home ownership. However, the 1933 Home Owners Loan Corporation (HOLC) program to curb mortgage defaults or foreclosures during the Depression did little to help black home owners. Of the tens of thousands of mortgages that were refinanced, less than 1 percent were held by blacks. Equally important, the HOLC created a racially discriminatory system of property appraisal that prevented almost all black home owners from having access to government mortgages and, ultimately, to the suburbs. Explicit in the procedures of evaluation was the actual and potential racial composition of a community. Communities that were already black or were changing to predominantly black were designated as undesirable for HOLC financing. Communities were assigned colors on residential or census tract maps: all-white communities, the most desirable, were colored green [for growth]; racially mixed or all-black communities, the least desirable, were colored red [for danger].

The Federal Housing Authority (FHA) was established in 1934 to bolster the American economy by underwriting housing construction. This was the advent of the modern mortgage system, which has enabled individuals to purchase homes with small down payments, reasonable interest rates, long-term repayment, and full amortization. Unfortunately for blacks, the FHA adopted the HOLC approval system. The FHA *Underwriting Manual* stated, "If a neighborhood is to retain stability, it is necessary that properties shall continue to be occupied by the same social and racial classes." Thus, official government policy supported bigoted white finance company executives, realtors, appraisers, and community residents.

In summary, the national housing gap between blacks and whites has, over time, actually widened through federal housing policies, the most important of which have been government programs that subsidized single-family detached housing. Since the Emancipation Proclamation, over thirty-five million families, almost all white, have acquired government-subsidized housing, with black Americans largely restricted to inferior, urban housing.

Residential Segregation

Although ethnic-group segregation is historical in nature, the acculturation experiences of blacks in America have been very different from the historical experiences of people of European descent. From the 1800s to about 1960, many urban neighborhoods in the United States underwent considerable population change as wave after wave of different immigrant groups moved through them. They were the scene of a large exodus of established immigrants concurrent with a larger influx of new ones. Robert Park described this phenomenon as an *ecological invasion:*

> An urban area may witness a series of invasions within a relatively short time. The near west side of Chicago, for example,...was first settled by Czechs, but when the Jews began to crowd into the area after the Chicago fire in 1877...[the Czechs] forsook the region for more desirable quarters.... The Jewish residents had hardly become firmly entrenched when the Italians came. Between 1910 and 1918 more than half the Jewish population...moved to other parts of the city. The coming of Negroes provided an added stimulus to the Jewish exodus (Gist and Halbert 1956, 280).

Neighborhoods not only changed in ethnicity but also in socioeconomic characteristics. Generally, they changed from white to black and from middle class to lower class. Even though first- and second-generation European immigrants often lived in segregated housing, the degree of their residential segregation declined rapidly after the peak levels of immigration in the early twentieth century. White ethnic enclaves were temporary and, to a large extent, optional. For black Americans and other people of color, segregation has been perennial and, for the most part, involuntary.

Based on housing patterns, most blacks are persona non grata in white America. They are the "opposite race," "the enemy." When blacks move into neighborhoods occupied by whites, social scientists frequently use the war term *invasion* but when whites move into neighborhoods occupied by blacks, reflecting their superiority, they call this *integration.*

The assertion is sometimes made that residential segregation is mainly the result of differences in economic status rather than discriminatory behavior and race. But the fact is, economic differences between blacks and whites have little effect on housing segregation. "You can graduate from the nation's most prestigious universities," a black executive told a group of black high school honor students, "but you cannot graduate from your blackness."

If economics alone determined where people lived, wealthy people of all races would be neighbors, and poor people of all races would be neighbors. They usually are not. Well-to-do blacks usually live far apart from well-to-do whites; poor whites and poor blacks generally do not share the same residential areas. Nor do economic factors explain the small number of blacks who live in the suburbs. U.S. census data reveal that in most metropolitan areas the suburbs are occupied by whites of all socioeconomic levels but are generally inaccessible to blacks in any significant number, no matter how well off. Again, if people were residentially distributed according to their income rather than their racial identity, most suburban neighborhoods would be racially mixed.

In local and national surveys more than three-fourths of black respondents have expressed a preference for racially mixed neighborhoods (W. A. V. Clark 1992; Farley et al. 1979; Lake 1981). While these preferences do not tell us where black families would actually live if given the choice, they indicate a rejection of their lifelong experiences in segregated housing. Certainly, many upwardly mobile blacks seem to be boxed into black slums.

The development of black ghettos in the United States, then, was not mainly the result of poverty, nor do most blacks continue to live there by choice. Instead, predominantly black communities are significantly the result of exclusion by whites. Langston Hughes catches the irony:

Here I come!
Been saving all my life
To get a nice home
For me and my wife.
White folks flee—
As soon as you see
My problems
And me!
Neighborhood's clean,
But the house is old,
Prices are doubled
When I get sold:
Still I buy.
White folks fly—
Soon as you spy
My wife
And I!
Next thing you know,
Our neighbors all colored are.
The candy store's
Turned into a bar:
White folks have left
The whole neighborhood
To my black self.
White folks flee!
Still—there is me!

White folks, fly!
Here am I!

                    —"Little Song on Housing"
                         Langston Hughes

Black parents who voluntarily live in predominantly black communities often do so fully realizing that their children are likely to attend schools less well staffed and equipped than predominantly white schools and that their neighborhoods are likely to be poorly policed and unlikely to receive adequate city and private services. Living in a predominantly black neighborhood, however, does provide respite from the racism outside.

The choice to live in a predominantly white community is not a panacea either. Along with better-staffed and adequately equipped schools also come bigoted white teachers, administrators, parents, and students. Blacks who move into historically white areas are often told directly and indirectly that they are neither wanted nor welcome there. Crass rejection is illustrated by such taunts as "You niggers don't belong in this neighborhood." A more sophisticated form of rejection is seen in the hateful stares of white people who resent blacks merely walking in a "white" neighborhood. White people referred to as "poor white trash" can understand the impact of such rejection, but they too usually reject blacks. A black dentist was almost reduced to tears when he recalled, "I was cursed out by people who couldn't afford the monthly payment on my car.... And they didn't want me living in their apartment complex." A black professor described his experience moving from a central city black neighborhood to a medium-sized southwestern white suburban community:

> We were the first black family to own property in the city. A cross was burned on our lawn. Garbage was thrown on our property. Our cars were spattered with raw eggs. Obscene telephone calls at all hours of the day encouraged us to leave town. The police frequently stopped me and inquired about my reason for being in the neighborhood. But the cruel-

est things happened to my children. Some of their peers called them "niggers," "apes," "shines," "jungle bunnies," and "coons" and told them that we should go back to Africa. The burned cross was easily removed, the cars were quickly cleaned, unwanted telephone calls were monitored by the police and the culprits were punished, and the police became our protectors instead of our hasslers. But nothing could be done to remove from my children's memories the cruel treatment they received.

Culprits

Responsibility for housing discrimination against blacks can be laid at the feet of many culprits, including government, private agencies, and individuals. It has been nearly two decades since the enactment of federal legislation to prohibit housing discrimination, but causal practices are still rampant. They usually take subtle, covert forms. The policies and practices of various federal government agencies have been particularly important in perpetuating discrimination. Blacks, for example, still pay higher rates than whites for FHA and VA home loans, and federal banking regulators are often lax in monitoring discriminatory mortgage practices.

Since the establishment of federal housing programs during the Depression, the ghetto housing patterns created by formal policies have become almost impossible to alter. Black ghettos grew simultaneously with discrimination and segregation in education, employment, and human services. They became such a fundamental feature of American life that they were generally taken for granted, viewed as natural forms of social organization, and even cited as evidence that blacks prefer to "live with their own kind."

Whatever gains blacks make relative to whites in obtaining jobs and reasonable incomes, they tend to lag far behind whites in comparable housing. Past discriminatory practices of the FHA and other housing agencies still appear to exert an influence on housing patterns in the nation's metropolitan areas. According to 1990 U.S. Census Bureau data, 67 percent of white Americans owned their own homes, compared with 43 percent of black Americans. In May 1988 the *Atlanta Journal and Constitution* published Bill Dedman's Pulitzer Prize-winning series, "The Color of Money," that documented discriminatory mortgage-lending practices. Other reports corroborated Dedman's thesis: black applicants are rejected at a greater rate than whites, even when economic resources are comparable (Acuna 1989; Brenner and Spayd 1993; Epstein 1996; *Federal Reserve Bulletin* 1992; Lehman 1991; *Los Angeles Times* 1989; Zuckoff 1992). Data from the Federal Financial Institutions Examination Council are also disturbing: in 1996, 48.1 percent of blacks who applied for home mortgages were denied compared with 21.1 percent of whites. In some instances, poor white applicants are given loans denied to blacks with considerably more income and better credit ratings.

Not all of the discrimination that results in residential segregation is attributable to federal housing agencies. Discrimination in the provision of public services such as paved roads, regular trash collection, and new schools is a standard practice in communities that have identifiable black subcommunities. This is a not-too-subtle way residential areas for blacks are further demarcated and stigmatized.

White landlords, home owners, real estate agents, and lenders are other culprits and account for most racial segregation in housing. Sometimes all four groups make a concerted effort to exclude blacks from certain neighborhoods or communities. Of the four, realtors and their agents, as the institutional gatekeepers of housing opportunities, are mainly responsible for steering blacks away from or into certain housing. Financial institutions cooperate by rejecting black applications to purchase property in white or predominantly white areas.

It is illegal to engage in "blockbusting," persuading property owners to sell or rent housing by telling them that minority groups are moving into the neighborhood. Nor can moneylenders legally deny blacks home loans or make terms or conditions for loans different from those required of whites. The courts have spoken quite clearly to real estate agency managers and agents on the issue of *responsibility*. And under the doctrine of *respondeat superior* (let the master answer for wrongful acts of his agent), they must obey the law. Yet these laws are routinely ignored. Various federal government documents indicate that there are over two million incidents of race-based housing discrimination every year.

The final culprits of housing discrimination are racial prejudice and fear. In the end no laws—federal, state, or local—have been able to dispel the fear that many white people have of blacks moving next door or into the same block. The expectation by whites that a neighborhood will become black leads them to take individual and collective action that ensures the outcome. When this happens, illegal housing covenants against sales or rentals to blacks are exercised, panic-selling tactics stimulate white residents to leave, and potential white buyers from other parts of the city are steered away from the neighborhood because it is "turning," "changing," or "going black."

Segregated Schools

Education is a pervasive government-organized activity that reaches into every community. The institutionalization of racially discriminatory practices throughout public school systems is a substantial cause as well as effect of other racial practices. Most children are profoundly influenced by their school experiences, not only in terms of formal academic learning but also in the development of a sense of self and a philosophy about social life and acceptable behavior.

There is an interdependent relationship between school segregation and neighborhood segregation. Each reinforces the other. Policies that encourage the development and continuation of racially identifiable schools foster residential segregation, which in turn fosters school segregation. The racial composition of student bodies and school staffs creates a racial identity of the surrounding neighborhood. In many urban areas school-attendance zones define the boundaries between neighborhoods. Most home buyers who have school-age children use school-attendance zones as a guide in their selection of a residence. Therefore, realtors take particular care to "sell" schools as an aspect of residence: school zones are often listed in classified advertisements for homes in the newspaper. These zones covertly identify the racial character of neighborhoods.

Change in the racial identity of a neighborhood school can influence the pace of change in the racial composition of its residential area. A school with a stable racial mix connotes to residents and potential residents that they will not be forsaken by school authorities. School policies can help stabilize neighborhoods and generate confidence in continued stability. Most whites, however, do not remain in or move into a neighborhood whose schools have a large or increasing proportion of black students or staff, because they believe that such schools will be neglected by school officials, resulting in a lowering of the schools' academic standards and social status.

The Challenge

It has been more than fifty years since Gunnar Myrdal's (1944) seminal study, *An American Dilemma*, was published. If there is a common theme emerging from the hundreds of studies since Myrdal's book, it is a reaffirmation of his observation that racial problems in America are many, varied, and intractable. Residential segregation, school segregation, employment discrimination, and discriminatory acts of city, county, state, and federal officials are linked to form a complex pattern of social privilege and denial based on race. The general picture of the United States as a place of prosperity and abundance is marred by the fact that all Americans do not share in it. A disproportionate number of black Americans constitute a subculture made up of individuals without the education or technical skills needed to gain admission to mainstream American life. The wrongheaded belief held by countless whites that because of their racial identity blacks have their own place in America, and that they had better stay there, is an obstacle to positive race relations. Upon close examination, it is evident that social class, although fraught with problems, is a better determinant of one's initial place. A requisite for improving black-white relations in the United States is a change in attitudes. The majority of white Americans must believe that blacks have the same inalienable rights as whites to attend quality schools, get a decent job, and otherwise be treated as full citizens. The next chapters of this book will suggest ways to make this happen.

Chapter 5

Teaching Black Children

Implications of Unequal Educational Opportunities

Poverty and unequal educational opportunities in the United States are by no means confined to black communities, and discrimination and prejudice against those who are different from white Americans are not directed only at black Americans (any American boy or girl who has completed grade school in a rural community and has then moved to an urban community to attend high school knows how difficult it is to become a member of the ingroup). Nevertheless, poverty in cities inhabited largely by black Americans presents a more difficult challenge than rural poverty. Discrimination on racial or ethnic grounds is more difficult to contend with than is discrimination on social grounds, a problem also more acute in the cities.

Although few would doubt the existence of an urban crisis in the United States, there seem to be no easy solutions in sight. It is widely recognized, however, that it will take the combined and coordinated efforts of many people—black and white—to solve the crisis, and the schools are expected to play a major role. It is also generally acknowledged that the schools cannot fulfill this role by trying to impose educational programs designed for middle-class white children on black children whose home environments have not prepared them for such programs.

In an attempt to resolve this dilemma, expedients such as racial desegregation and compensatory programs specifically designed for underclass children have been developed and tried. Nevertheless, these efforts have, for the most part, failed. Racial desegregation has not proceeded as rapidly as had been expected or been as successful as many had hoped, and it has been beset by unforeseen problems. Indeed, there are now more racially segregated public schools than there were in 1971, when the U.S. Supreme Court ruled in *Swann vs. Charlotte-Mecklenburg Board of Education* that forced busing can be used to achieve racial desegregation. Compensatory education programs such as Head Start, initiated in the 1960s, can to some extent compensate for the absence of opportunities for learning in desegregated schools, but black children who have been in such programs have generally fallen behind white children when they have entered schools with no provisions for differentiated instruction. It can be said that education in predominantly black schools still presents a dismal picture, characterized by old buildings, inadequately prepared teachers, and a high percentage of dropouts. Although cities, states, and the federal government have spent huge sums on urban education programs, problems continue to mount.

Nowhere is the failure of traditional educational practices more obvious than in school subjects dealing with the transmission of the heritage of history. The richness of language, the cultivation of aesthetic response, and the desire to create a better nation are all societal objectives which school can and should foster in order to give each student an appreciation of those values which are the glory of civilization. But more than just an appreciation of the Western past and a knowledge of traditional literary classics is needed to encourage African American creativity. To neglect the contributions of non-Western cultures in a rapidly changing world is to foster unproductive ethnocentrism.

It would appear from the results of national assessment data that many of the works of literature judged to be classics by both educational authorities and test makers are not relevant to the experience of most black students. No wonder then that it is the literature questions that are most often called culturally biased. The fact remains that a large number of black students, for whatever reason, do not experience many of the aesthetic joys associated with literature which are daily being nurtured in white students. While some black students visit a library often and spend free time reading, it is apparent from national assessment data that, as a group, the quality and subject matter of their reading does substantially less to broaden their horizons, develop their writing and reading skills, and cultivate their aesthetic responses than does the reading of white students in affluent suburbs. In fact, it might be concluded that instead of contributing to their educational growth, much of black students' reading material makes few demands on their own thoughts and feelings. Worse still, most of the books they are inclined to read give them a distorted view of their cultural heritage. We do not need assessment results to tell us that the average black student's opportunities to visit a great museum, hear a fine musician, converse with an inspiring poet, or enjoy the performance of a professional drama group are far fewer than for the average white student. Nonetheless, despite all its faults, in the black community education is still believed to be the best way to escape second-class citizenship. And parents continue to make great sacrifices to send their children to school because they believe that education is a great equalizer of cultures—the balance wheel of economic and social mobility. W. E. B. Du Bois (1903) wrote:

> Teach thinkers to think—a needed knowledge in a day of loose and careless logic; and they whose lot is gravest must have the carefulest training to think alright.... Teach thinkers to think; make carpenters of carpenters, and philosophers of philosophers, and

fops of fools. Nor can we pause here. We are training not isolated men—nay, a group within a group.
And the final product of our training must be neither a psychologist nor a brickmason, but a man.
And to make men, we must have ideals, broad, pure,
and inspiring ends of living... (72).

Central to educating our citizens is the development of
articulate and proficient writers and speakers, a goal of
education in all literate, technically advanced societies.
Where there is an inability to adequately communicate, a
sense of isolation results, and so too does a sense of the
lack of power for self-expression and self-assertion. The
economic and political implications are mind-boggling.

Economic Implications

Few educators today would question that the period since
World War II in the United States has been one of an increasing correlation between formal education and economic status. Current American history books still devote
at least one chapter to extolling those citizens who became wealthy, influential, and beloved, though born in
humble surroundings in which there was little opportunity for more than the most rudimentary learning. That
world of economic mobility, however, is as far removed
from today's reality as is the world of log cabins and prai-
rie schooners. Yet it is largely upon these same economic
myths that American public education, at least at the elementary and secondary levels, still rests.

If economic status is conditioned by formal education
to an appreciable degree, then it is obvious that most black
students who aspire to succeed compete under a crippling
burden of inequality. Inner-city black children, if one is to
judge correctly from the national assessment data, will do
well if they manage to secure and hold a blue-collar job in
the decreasing job markets of inner-city America, let alone
find employment which will allow them to rise above their
parents economically and give their own children certain
fundamental benefits. It is more likely that black students

will become unskilled workers than computer program-
mers and far more likely that they will work for someone
else rather than manage their own business or pursue a
profession. The prospects for their children are not much
brighter and may be even more bleak.

In the struggle for upward economic mobility, the majority of black children begin, whatever their native gifts,
at an educational disadvantage when compared with white
children in all environments—small and medium-sized cities, suburban areas, and, most especially, large urban areas. At a manifest disadvantage in the skills of reading
and writing, relatively untutored in basic science, and less
interested in civic matters than most others, they predictably become economic failures.

Political Implications

Political writers and commentators never seem to tire of
telling the American people that true democracy rests with
an informed public. If this is true, national assessment data
should make us anxious about the future of representa-
tive government. In a democracy, where an informed con-
stituency is requisite for stable self-government, the political implications of schools neglecting black population
pockets can readily be seen. Below the national average in
reading, black inner-city students are less likely to read
publications that can give them the facts which enable them
to make informed political decisions and to work for
change. Deficient in writing skills, they can be expected to
write few, if any, letters to their local newspaper to draw
attention to a problem which affects their lives and the
lives of their children. Less concerned with civic participation than other people, the average black inner-city person is a predictable target for political candidates who
promise simple solutions to complex problems. Black citizens who are unaware of their rights or too unschooled in
political techniques to protect themselves are obviously
vulnerable to others who seek to manipulate them.

The key to participatory democracy is found in traditional political channels; yet if these channels are not used by certain segments of our population because of lack of knowledge, the concept of democracy is at best an idealized, unfulfilled dream. Unable or unwilling to become involved in the democratic process, a disproportionate number of black citizens are more likely than their white counterparts to leave untapped their collective powers, which, when exercised properly, could lead to more control of their local, state, and national governments.

Teachers Matter

The percentage of well-qualified white teachers in schools with black students in their classes is increasing, and the more effective of these realize that in order to be successful, particularly in teaching black and other minority students, they cannot overlook the cultural backgrounds, needs, and problems of their students. Without a doubt the problems that many of these students bring to school are enmeshed in race, cultural norms, and social class. These problems, as well as those they acquire while in school, affect their ability to profit from school experiences. An effective teacher is able to assist students in understanding and resolving, or at least coping with, such problems.

A teacher can view a black student from two perspectives: as intelligent, an asset to the class, and likely to succeed; or as stupid, a troublemaker, and a born loser. At some point in the semester, most students are able to determine their teachers' expectations of them, and they learn to play appropriate roles. Teachers' attitudes are that powerful.

Change tends to come slowly and to exact a toll on teachers. A white elementary school student teacher wrote,

I am so far from having adequate training that it is ridiculous. I am, very simply, not prepared to teach. Not *these* children. They have been battered by life until they are no more than pulsating open wounds. Then I—a healthy dose of salt—come along. It isn't fair to them.

I see how my own rearing has given me certain expectations about children...all too high....

These children are so angry. And they take it out on each other: they taunt one another, poke, hit, tear papers, wad them up, scribble on them. How do you teach them not to hurt each other? They get angry and I get angry. And I don't know what to do with either of us.

Mrs. B. [the principal] says to force them to read when we are in the reading circle and they don't want to. That's a good way to make them hate it. I usually say, "Well, we are here to read; but would you rather go to your seat?" They never say yes because they know Mrs. B. will make them return anyway. But I'd let them go. So then I say, "Perhaps you'll feel like reading later." And I do ask them later. If they still say no, I point out that I will help them.

Mrs. B. says you have to keep your thumb on them all the time.

My personality requires order. I need some sort of order in the room. I wish I knew how to let them know that even if I can't help them right now, I will later. I think they have experienced failure all their lives and are afraid that this is just more of the same.

I wish there could be some time for them to talk to me, and I to them. There are so many things that they need to say to me. And they need to hug me and drag me down to their level for a wet kiss. I wonder if a talk time in the morning would work.

How much do they need to learn about getting along? Mrs. B. is quite strict. Her children will be courteous and polite to everyone or she will know the reason why. She forces them to apologize for any misbehavior to me, for walking in front of someone, stepping on someone's toes, etc.

I wonder if a child's pouting is not his attempt to curb his aggressive tendencies. This pouting always takes place when his goal has been blocked and he is angry. They seem to funnel their anger into a pout. Here again is my own rearing: I was always sternly admonished for both pouting and whining. As a result, I find that I dislike the children in my room who do this.

I guess the one I like best is the one who tells me off. He will come up to me and say, "I'm not coming back to school. You make me mad. I'm not coming back...the way you act." Out of the mouths of babes! It's damned hard being a good teacher.

There is no question about it: teachers matter very much. Unfortunately, the preponderance of research indicates that few colleges of education are adequately preparing teachers for cultural diversity. A discomforting paradox is that within two decades, if the current pattern continues, 48 percent of the public school student population will be ethnic minority children, but less than 3 percent of the teachers will be minorities. Even more disturbing, surveys conducted by the Carnegie Foundation (1988) note that while most of the white teachers want to develop positive relations with black students, they do not succeed. They have little knowledge of black people, and as the gap between the teachers' and the students' values and lifestyles widens, increased alienation occurs.

Personal Characteristics

Teachers who feel at ease in their jobs tend to be successful; they create a classroom atmosphere conducive to learning. Those who do not feel comfortable make their classroom a repressive place for students and for themselves. Since most white teachers have experienced little or no contact with black people prior to becoming teachers, their concern about establishing rapport is reasonable. Many white high school teachers, especially women, are anxious about how black students will respond to their appearance, age, or personality. There is the matter of teacher dress, for example: what should the teacher wear to class? If she dresses too casually, or too conservatively, she may create an unfavorable or undesirable student response. Or she may be concerned about hairstyle. If the teacher's hairstyle is not acceptable to her students, she may be the object of ridicule and laughter.

A great many beginning high school teachers worry about looking too young and may doubt their ability to control black students who are near their own age. In addition to appearance and age, white teachers may have some worries about their personality. Will they be compatible with their students? Will their sense of humor be understood? Should they be friendly or reserved? Should they be humorous or dry? Should they be authoritarian or democratic? Can they convey self-confidence?

Certainly white teachers should be concerned about their appearance, but the truth is that most black students are not too concerned about how youthful a teacher of any color looks. Nor are they obsessed with any great preference for personal attractiveness among white teachers. Although studies indicate that many black students condone extreme behavior for themselves, most of them do not want teachers to deviate too far from acceptable middle-class norms. Signs of deviation are seen in "far-out" hairstyles, uncoordinated clothes, or decrepit automobiles. "Dressing up," for example, is better than "dressing down."

For the most part, black students are concerned with the following questions:

1. Is the teacher able to put students at ease? Black students, unlike white students, tend to be apprehensive about pleasing white people.
2. Is the teacher able to empathize with and show understanding of the students and to convey positive expectations? Unlike most white students, black students as a whole need constant reassurance that they can do well in school if they apply themselves.

3. Is the teacher's voice pleasant, or is it harsh and irritating to the listener? Most often, black students are yelled at in their homes.
4. Does the teacher take a positive approach in his or her classroom techniques? Unlike most white students, whose upbringing centers on positive reinforcement from parents, most black children are socialized through harsh, often negative parental action.
5. Is the teacher able to present material in an interesting and meaningful way that holds the attention of students? Having few or no meaningful interactions with white people before interacting with white teachers, many black students believe what they are told by their relatives—that white people are boring.
6. Is the teacher sincere? This means sincerely committed to teaching black children.
7. Does the teacher's classroom bearing suggest that he or she enjoys teaching, or does it appear that teaching is just a job? Most black students initially believe that only the white teachers' salaries bring them into contact with black people, and if they could do something else and avoid teaching, they would.
8. Does the teacher exhibit a sense of humor appropriate to the class setting? White students are concerned about white teachers' ability to display dominant society humor. Black students prefer white teachers who can "get down" [appreciate humor that is black in origin and meaning].
9. Does the teacher have a real concern for all of the students? Does he or she appear to be sensitive to cultural differences between white and black students? White students tend to be individualistic—concerned about themselves; generally black students are collectivistic—concerned about their black classmates.
10. Does the teacher know and understand the subject matter or is he or she bluffing and pretending to know it, and is the material relevant to the students' lives?

"Understanding" for black students means not only knowing course material but being able to relate it to their lives.

Some of these questions are difficult for teachers to answer about themselves. Add to this the fact that black students will make certain judgments about their teachers in the first several days of school, so first impressions need to be good ones. A businesslike manner tempered with a sense of humor can contribute much to black students' acceptance of white teachers. Of course, it is possible, though rare, for a white teacher to be effective even after making an extremely poor initial impression on black students. Nonetheless, the probability of success in the classroom is enhanced if the teacher begins with student acceptance.

Black students need teachers who will appropriately touch, smile, and otherwise interact with them. White teachers who view black students as if they have highly contagious diseases, whether consciously or subconsciously, try to avoid contact with them. "These teachers ain't worth jack [nothing]," a black student remarked. He was specifically referring to a white teacher who habitually sprayed disinfectant around the classroom and wiped all the books and pencils with tissues before accepting them from black students. Also suspect are teachers who routinely schedule an "I understand your problems" lecture. In fact black students frequently test this pretense of empathy by contriving forced interactions. Many teachers fail, as did the one who jumped back in horror when a shabbily dressed black girl rushed up to receive the warmth that had been promised in the lecture.

Effective teachers establish positive relationships before focusing on course content. Close contact with small numbers of black students affords opportunities for white teachers to reach students on a personal level. White teachers may also gain a degree of early acceptance through evidence of their interest in students' cocurricular activities.

Their presence and participation as spectators at school musicals or athletic contests, for instance, will convince students of their interest and involvement in all aspects of the students' school life.

Establishing Relationships and Working Effectively

A teacher who is perceived as an outsider will have less influence than one who is believed to be part of the school and community, and, initially, white teachers in predominantly black schools are outsiders. Within each class, however, are students who can help teachers gain acceptance, and experienced teachers know the mediatory power of informal student leaders. If a peer-group leader does not like a teacher, that teacher is likely to experience great class resistance. In inner-city schools the informal leader is frequently in a gang; in white schools, only rarely. When cultivating student acceptance, however, teachers must be careful, as they must also with white children, not to show favoritism, since it can result in a student's being labeled a teacher's pet. Not only will this reduce the effectiveness of the liaison role the student is capable of playing, but the student so labeled will also lose status. Most white teachers unwisely overlook low-achieving black students as potential sources of entry into classroom acceptance. A white teacher with ten years of experience reluctantly admitted, "When it comes to understanding my black students and their community, it is I who am culturally deprived."

The first step in establishing rapport with students is to help them relax. In order to do this, the teacher must be relaxed, and if a white teacher is worried about being verbally or physically attacked, he or she will not relax. There are certainly enough movies and television specials showing violence in inner-city schools to perpetuate this fear.

Fearful teachers lose control of the classroom. Black and white students alike interpret a teacher's lack of control as an abdication of adult responsibility and authority. Inept teachers alienate both groups. In addition to amplifying the problem of control, these teachers also create interracial problems. Such disorder is at its zenith in predominantly black schools.

Black students are anxious about their initial contact with white teachers, too. For many low-achieving black students the mere presence of white people of any kind produces feelings of great discomfort. During these stressful periods, school assignments or conversation related to such assignments may panic the students. Teachers must learn when to slow the pace and talk about nonacademic subjects. A few minutes of small talk can often reduce the stress. A warm, informal, down-to-earth chat with each student is also critical to establishing rapport.

Some black students are extremely defensive in class with white teachers, and those who behave this way are usually merely protecting their egos; disproportionate defensiveness often indicates a lack of security. Rationalization, reaction formation (distancing oneself from socially undesirable persons who are like themselves), overcompensation, and other defensive behaviors are ways black students seek to maintain their psychological balance. Continued feelings of rejection often result in inappropriate behavior.

One African American student imagined that all white teachers disliked him. To protect himself, he withdrew from voluntary contact with them. When one substitute white teacher asked him, "Why don't you like me?" he answered, "Because you don't like me. You touch and smile at the white kids but you never touch or smile at me." When discussing this exchange with another white teacher, she said,

> You got to be careful around them [black students]. If you smile too much at the guys, they'll think you're coming on to them. Some of those little studs are in heat all the time. You shouldn't do anything to en-

courage them. The girls are just as bad. The only difference is they mistake your smile for friendship and want to talk to you all the time. The best thing we [white teachers] can do is to show them no emotions.

She was talking about students in the fifth grade. We can only speculate about how she would treat black teenagers. Her treatment of white students when she was a substitute in an all-white school was very different: "I just loved being there. The kids were so clean and polite. Just the thought of them brings a smile to my face. There were no problems at that school. Not like these kids."

Issues that center on race or ethnicity cause white teachers and black students to overreact. Often it is difficult to sift out fact from fiction, objectivity from subjectivity. The use of excessive ego defenses by students is disturbing to teachers who are unaware of having done anything to elicit such behavior. Most white teachers want their black students to like them, but, as a teary-eyed African American girl said, "They've got some strange ways of showing it." A smile or a nod is a small but effective way to communicate acceptance. This is especially true in classes containing a large number of passive or frustrated black students. White teachers assigned to these classes should not themselves become passive or frustrated by the thought of trying to teach them.

Communication

The willingness of black students to interact with white teachers is, as I've said earlier, affected in part by the value of the relationship (what it can do for them) and in part by the belief that only through a cooperative effort can they achieve certain goals. The old "Do what I tell you because I am the teacher" approach seldom works. All students find abundant ways to misbehave when they are unwilling to accept communication and direction from teachers. They can sabotage the educational process by disobeying orders, chewing gum, talking without asking permission, neglecting to hand in written assignments, withdrawing, becoming aggressive, or doing only what they are ordered to do. However, when black students behave this way toward white teachers, the sabotage usually escalates to a "get whitey" atmosphere, taking on mean racial overtones. Open, honest expressions of feelings obviate the necessity for these reactions. An open dialogue, however, is not synonymous with automatic teacher approval. Teachers should make it clear that permitting candid expression of feelings does not mean that they necessarily approve of the feelings verbalized or the actions surrounding them. Such a conversation or dialogue will probably be a new experience for black students. Seldom do they have the opportunity in school to talk about things of personal interest to them; therefore, when they are asked to participate in candid classroom discussion, most black students will be unprepared and hesitant. If the subject is race, they will be even more reluctant to talk. Once they start talking, however, the danger is that they may not stop! Every student has something to contribute to classroom discussions. Good teachers are good listeners; they learn to listen with all their senses, not merely their ears. To maintain some control over the process, they establish time limitations and ground rules for courteous behavior, and they are skilled in facilitating discussion and resolving conflict. When this is not the case, episodes like the following will be repeated many times:

> A white history teacher of an integrated class was discussing slavery. After his final lecture, the students were asked to present their opinions. A white student gave an emotional appeal for understanding the position of the plantation owners. A black student sitting next to her became visibly upset and called her names: "racist," "bigot." The teacher, sensing that a fight could erupt, moved between the students,

putting his hands on the black student's shoulder in an effort to restrain her. She pushed his hands away, cautioning him to keep his "white hands" off her. Angrily, she accused him of being a white racist and admonished him to talk to his "racist friend" [the white student], who started the argument. In a calm voice, the teacher should have (1) apologized to the black student for touching her, (2) asked the black student to apologize to the white student for calling her derogatory names, (3) asked the white student to explain her reason for defending slavery, and (4) let the class discuss the importance of tolerance of opinions.

The first concerns expressed by black students may not be the ones that teachers want to discuss. Like all other aspects of teaching, classroom discussions should start where the students are emotionally concerned. Unemployment, family illness, racism, and neighborhood violence may be of more immediate interest than Shakespeare or the Great Depression, and if students' issues are ignored, the issues become material for daydreaming. Black students are not likely to accept a white teacher's lesson plan until their concerns are recognized and accepted as valid. Whatever problems these students bring to school are exacerbated when teachers refuse to listen to them.

Channels of communication are opened only when teachers uncritically accept each student's effort to communicate, even if it is only nonverbal. This requires learning about the students, especially becoming familiar with their ways of communicating. While the effects of environmental limitations cannot be completely erased, they can be ameliorated by offering students hope in place of despair and confidence in place of insecurity. One white teacher got her poor black students' cooperation in part because, as she told them, she believed "You live in poverty but your mind can be rich with knowledge."

Most black students are also very sensitive to what teachers do *not* say. "She never told me I did good work," one student lamented. Another said, "He [the teacher] always talked about himself and his children. It's like we didn't exist."

Most black children come to school curious, but within a few years most of them have lost their academic curiosity. The attention of a child has been compared to a wild animal that must be lured, caught, and held. Along with being a place for honest dialogue, the classroom should be a place of interest, concentration, and involvement. Some students—especially those who witness drive-by shootings and other deviant behaviors—are impulsive, hyperactive, and diffuse in behavior; their attention span is short, shifting from one thing to another. Others are apathetic, low in energy output, and passive. Every child exhibits these behaviors at one time or another; it is the disproportionate number of blacks who do so that makes it difficult for teachers to do well with them. Black students who pull back from white teachers are frightened, and those who are aggressive are angry.

Managing Negative Feelings

Effective teachers are able to manage students' negative feelings. While they may not be able to deal with all students equally, they try to minimize unfair treatment and maximize fair treatment. Getting to know black students does not always alter white teachers' negative attitudes toward black people, but it does allow them to respond more objectively to the students' classroom performance. While it would be ideal, a teacher need not love black children in order to teach them; understanding and empathy as well as teaching and learning can still occur. Effective white teachers realize that regardless of a child's background, he or she deserves the chance to learn and to be respected as an individual. Gloria Ladson-Billings (1994) called these teachers the "dreamkeepers."

The importance of managing negative attitudes is underscored by the fact that within the classroom the teacher and informal student leaders are the primary sources of approval and disapproval. Inner-city teachers quickly learn that in loco parentis gives them the opportunity to be forbidding, punishing, and threatening—or understanding, rewarding, and reassuring. Similar to white students, black students react to their teachers' approval and disapproval in various ways. Approval encourages some students to seek higher levels of achievement but causes others to rest on their past achievements, whereas disapproval usually lowers aspirations or prompts students to stop trying altogether. Believing that they will not do well in school if the teacher is white, many black students desperately need to be told that they can do well. "It's a *prejudice* thing," a black student said when challenged to explain why inner-city black students as a whole do poorly in classes taught by white teachers. When the same student was told that most inner-city black students do not fare much better with black teachers, he shrugged and replied, "That's a *Uncle Tom* thing."

Inner-city teachers generally distribute approval and disapproval in a consistent but inequitable manner. A few black "favorites," usually high achievers, receive the approval. Conversely, a larger number of students, usually low achievers, receive most of the disapproval, leaving the majority of the class, average achievers, out of the affection-rejection relationship. Not surprisingly, *high-blame, low-praise* black students make the worst classroom adjustment.

Things are not much better for black students in desegregated schools. Often low-achieving black students feel that they are not participants in the classroom dialogue. Instead, they feel like strangers visiting the school. In the words of a black student, "The teachers give the good kids [white students] all the attention…. They don't even know I'm in the class. But they know that the white kids are there…. They let them ask questions, answer questions, and get away with murder. Me, I just look cross-eyed and I get in trouble. So I wised up and stopped talking...."

It is difficult not to reject students who disrupt a class or who do not seem to care about doing the assignments. Sometimes these students will test their teachers (inside and outside of class) to see if they will turn against them, as did a black student wearing designer sunglasses when he walked into the school building and was stopped by Mr. C., his white math teacher.

"Hey, boy, what are you doing in school with those glasses on?" the teacher shouted.

The student grinned as a crowd began to form around them. "You talking to me, man?"

"Yes, I'm talking to you," the teacher responded. "Take off those glasses."

The student stopped smiling, glanced at the crowd, then clenched his fists and shouted, "If you so bad, you take 'em off."

They will ask teachers to give more of themselves than is humanly possible, thereby trying to justify their own negative acts. Throughout the initial trial period, effective teachers are not shocked by or hostile to students whose behaviors are irritating, abusive, or demanding. In many instances, the students are trying to make it easy for their teachers to reject them, but nothing positive happens when teachers diminish students' self-esteem—either in their own eyes or the eyes of their classmates.

Singling out students in front of their peers, criticizing them before their classmates, or otherwise embarrassing them are behaviors likely to produce additional problems. Black male students, in particular, who are treated in this manner will not want to succeed in school, and they will resent students who do. Teachers must master the art of controlling or correcting students without causing them to lose their self-esteem. Corrective action is best when it is perceived by students as being firm and fair. No student likes to lose face or to be ridiculed. Effective white teachers understand that while informal codes of conduct among black students allow them to harass each other, the teacher is not granted this privilege. Even if class members detest a particular student, they tend to support him or her against teachers whom they believe are unfair. The key issue is fairness.

Records, Reputations, and Expectations

All students have academic records and social reputations, both of which stick with them throughout their school career. Academic records consist of grades and test scores, while social reputations are an imprecise mixture of anecdotal records and rumors. Both are sources for gossip in the teachers' lounge. Many an "angel" or "devil" has been created from groundless rumor.

An illustration of how "angels" and "devils" are created is taken from a hall scene in an inner-city school. Huddled in a corner of the hall two white teachers were watching a small, undernourished black male walk past. "That's Buster," one of the teachers whispered. "He's the big devil who's always in trouble." Whether he was in fact always in trouble was unimportant to the wide-eyed beginning teacher, who felt privileged to have gotten the tip about Buster. "Forewarned," she sighed, "is forearmed." Later, she told of her experience with a white student and Buster.

> Buster and Jimmy were my problem students. Buster was a slow learner and Jimmy was a cute white boy. Fifteen-year-old Jimmy couldn't write and wouldn't read and I couldn't understand why. Anybody (white), I thought, with only the least amount of sense could do both. (I'm an extremely communication-oriented person, so it's as difficult for me to understand why some people can't read and write as it is for my engineer husband to understand why I can't do calculus.) I set out to prove that Jimmy's inability to succeed was only a matter of stubbornness on his

part. It didn't work. Later, Jimmy was placed in an apprenticeship program, where he learned to read and write.

Buster wasn't a person to me at all. He was sixteen, black, and had been passed along from grade to grade ever since he had been in the fifth grade. At one time or another, every teacher in the school had considered Buster a troublemaker. All became discouraged because he couldn't learn (this knowledge was first imparted to me in the teachers' lounge). I left Buster alone; I'd had enough personal challenges. The funny thing was that the other children liked him.

Teacher expectations are often the cause of low achievement among black students. Within most big-city schools a story persists about the principal who carefully informed his teachers at the beginning of the year that section A of a certain grade was the "accelerated" class and section B was the "slow" group. At the end of the year, the students in section A received grades much higher than those in section B. Ordinarily, this story would not be worth repeating. In several instances, however, the principals did not assign the students to ability groups according to past achievement scores but according to their ethnicity, with the predominantly black section being designated the slow-learning group. The teachers accepted the scores as infallible indicators of ability and taught accordingly. The "accelerated" students were given opportunities to excel, the "slow" students were not.

More than any other factor, low school achievement by black students is perpetuated by the low expectations of their teachers (Massey 1990; R. O. Washington 1982; White and Parham 1990). This negative attitude is usually an outgrowth of the notion of the biological inferiority of black Americans. Even though most teachers know that this notion is not true (and despite the vast literature detailing the environmental obstacles faced by black children), many white teachers continue to look mainly at their black students' accomplishments instead of their potential. Rather than break the failure pattern, as white suburban schools often do, most inner-city schools reinforce it. There is a strong temptation to accept a student's record or reputation as gospel. By so doing, teachers are relieved of the tiresome burden of reacting to students as individuals. Teachers who act as dogmatic judges of abilities condemn innocent children to a culture of poverty.

The best way to learn what students are like is to observe their behavior, watch how their peers interact with them, listen to their conversations, and let them tell you about themselves. Students' perception of their own behavior may provide important clues to their inability to do well in school. It is a rare experience for average black students to talk with white teachers who, instead of criticizing them, listen without judging. One of the major differences between an effective and an ineffective teacher is that the former listens with a sensitive ear and the latter, with a deaf ear.

Student records (if compiled fairly and sensitively) can provide valuable information from which teachers can piece together a portrait of the student. However, *no amount of prerecorded information is an adequate substitute for getting to know each student on a personal basis.*

Poor Black Male Students

Contrary to movie and television portrayals, most lower-class black male students are not *gangbangers* (members of juvenile gangs who participate in deviant activities) or *gangstas* ("outlaws" who reject white norms and white authority). Most of them are survivors—individuals who go along with gangbangers and gangstas in order to avoid being hassled by them. It is difficult, but not impossible, for teachers to turn these students around academically.

Because poor black males have more school adjustment problems than females, the following comments relate mainly to black males, who can be described in terms of five "focal concerns": trouble, toughness, smartness, excitement, and fate. These concerns are not unique to the low-income black community, but they seem to be accentuated there, and they play themselves out in the school environment.

Trouble is the dominant focal concern of poor black males. Needless to say, their neighborhoods have ample built-in trouble factors: high crime rate, drugs, hazardous buildings, overcrowded schools, and a disproportionate amount of unemployment and underemployment. Nevertheless, although they live in what may be called "marginal communities," most youths are not marginal people; they manage to adjust to these conditions. When they cannot adjust, however, they are overwhelmed, psychologically and physically, by their neighborhood.

A black male's peer-group status is usually based on his ability to risk trouble but to escape its consequences, thus maintaining a positive peer-group self-concept. Teachers, police, social workers, and other adults who demand law-abiding behavior merely add to the challenge to engage in law-violating behavior.

Toughness includes physical prowess, athletic ability, and proclaimed scorn for "white" things like art and literature and sometimes school achievement. Resisting activities they see as "sissy," many black male students are content to leave good grades to females. If a youth's peer group condones low school achievement, he will actively seek to conform to this norm. In fact, below-average school performance is a kind of initiation rite necessary for acceptance into some black groups. Thus, white teachers who are concerned that low-achieving black students of this sort have negative self-concepts need to keep in mind that low achievement in school can actually be a source of positive self-concept in the minds of such students when low achievement is a prerequisite for acceptance into peer groups.

Much of the emphasis on toughness in low-income black culture appears to be related to mother-centered homes. As noted in earlier chapters, black males continually seek to establish their masculine identity. In white culture, masculinity is closely tied to physical toughness but is usually limited to formally sanctioned games such as football, basketball, and hockey. On the other hand, poor black youths develop a physical toughness that is not directly related to formal games. For them, as noted above, it is a means of neighborhood survival. The black male who cannot defend himself in a fight or who does not have other things going for him becomes an easy mark for shakedowns, pranks, and other abuses. "Other things" include being able to run faster than peers, having tougher siblings or friends, or having a physical disability (children with disabilities are not acceptable targets of aggression). Thus poor black boys enter school culturally conditioned to disrupt orderly classrooms.

Perceptive teachers are able to provide classroom experiences that allow black males to be active participants without losing their masculine identity, their aura of toughness. High-achieving black males are sometimes asked to tutor male students who are having difficulty grasping the assignments. Such "brother-to-brother" aid is less embarrassing. Peer culture plays an important role in influencing student behavior in the classroom, and teachers who use it effectively can significantly enhance classroom learning. Students who feel humiliated in front of their peers are likely to become troublemakers—or school dropouts.

Smartness is the ability to outsmart someone else without being outsmarted or "conned" yourself. The hustlers in the neighborhood are considered to be smart because they work with their brains and not their backs. The list of smart people ranges from drug dealers to pimps, many of whom have big cars, lots of money, and pretty women as proof of their abilities. White teachers who make derogatory statements about such people usually do not score high with poor black youths. Such remarks come across as ignorant and also focus unneeded attention on deviant occupations.

Rarely is income a good selling point when teachers are competing with hustlers and criminals for a black student's acceptance. After all, a successful pimp or drug dealer earns considerably more than a schoolteacher. The real appeal of the middle class is its conformity to the dominant cultural norms. Such seemingly obvious attributes of middle-class occupations as "acceptance," "honesty," "legitimacy," and "prestige" should be emphasized, for they can become part of the lure for boys to seek middle-classness. And there is considerable parental support, especially from the mother, for them to seek legal occupations. Education is still perceived as the best way out of lower-class communities. It is the way to become "somebody."

Excitement is found in activities that flirt with trouble. Drinking, playing the "dozens" (see chapter 1), and being sexually promiscuous are some of the most common. Excitement, of course, is closely related to toughness. With community support, schools can provide poor black youths with alternative activities that are exciting but do not lead to trouble; bowling, ball games, wrestling matches, field trips, and concerts are examples. School fund-raising activities can be a means to underwrite these projects. Sometimes even a quiet talk is excitement enough. Many activities middle-class blacks find boring and "old hat" are new and exciting for poor blacks because they introduce them to an unfamiliar world.

Fate, most low-income black people believe, is the controlling factor in their lives. Believing that they are powerless to control their own lives, many black youths easily become discouraged. The world of middle-classness is a chess game in which they are pawns but rarely kings, knights, or rooks. It is the white man's world. Preoccupation with fate makes them vulnerable to "get-rich-quick" schemes. Gambling is believed to be the quickest and easiest way to "luck out." Although few poor people do "luck out," the hope of doing so provides excitement in an otherwise seemingly hopeless existence. White teachers who try to motivate poor black youths to seek middle-class occupations must convince them that they *can* control a portion of their lives by demonstrating the positive relationship between school success and job opportunities. Adult role models who have emerged from a background similar to that of the youths appear to have an edge in being able to make this comparison effectively.

The 1995 Million Man March was an example of black males engaging in a brother-to-brother activity designed to establish closer bonds, acknowledge responsibility for some of the plight of black Americans, and through this reconciliation dedicate themselves to community renewal. Hundreds of thousands of black men from all socioeconomic strata called each other "brother" and took a small step toward reclaiming their role as responsible black persons within their communities. For most participants, the march was a day of atonement. For some white Americans, it was an opportunity to see black males in a positive light.

But providing only black role models for black students overstates the importance of "race" and understates the importance of occupational competency. It is ironic that a democratic society's concern for incorporating into the mainstream a long-neglected minority group is adding to the philosophical basis of "black separatism." Some black students, for example, complain about white teachers offering courses in African American or black history. A typical remark is, "We need black people to teach black history. This will give us pride in being black. No white person can tell me about my past." A logical extension of this type of argument is that only whites can adequately teach and motivate whites. In fact, black students can use role models from all racial and ethnic groups.

Alienation and beyond Alienation

There is ample evidence to support the contention that most elementary and secondary schools are instruments of the dominant society. There is very little evidence to support the contention that they make system-wide initiatives in effecting social change. In other words, they reflect middle-class white America's social order. As a matter of fact, although the schools of this nation vary widely in location, type, organization, and other characteristics, when the subject is black students, their educational premises are remarkably similar: (1) native intelligence in children is measurable, (2) tests used to measure children's intelligence are reliable, (3) test results show that fewer black children than white children are capable of excelling in academic programs, and (4) most black students should be helped to adjust to their abilities and potentials and therefore be counseled into vocational and clerical curriculums rather than a college sequence.

Adding to conditions that lead to alienation, most elementary and secondary schools demand, and correctly so, that black students speak correct standard English as opposed to black English and calmly talk over their problems instead of being verbally demonstrative or physically aggressive. By now it should be evident why a large number of black students, particularly poor and underclass students, are alienated, a condition that is characterized by powerlessness, meaninglessness, normlessness, and isolation.

1. *Powerlessness.* Alienated black students often believe that they cannot, even through good behavior, achieve the educational goals they seek. These students feel controlled and manipulated by teachers and administrators. An extremely frustrated student might take his or her anger out on school property, as did the black student who wrote "damn, damn, damn" across the front of his books.

2. *Meaninglessness.* Alienated black students' classroom behavior frequently does not seem to have a relationship to the broader community. These students lack an understanding of how the school activities in which they are involved will lead to a job or a college scholarship. Equally distressing, alienated students are unclear as to what they ought to know in order to become better students. School rules and regulations seem to have no redeeming value.

3. *Normlessness.* In addition to believing that school rules and regulations are arbitrary, many black students are in schools where rules are not consistently enforced. There appears, then, to be no reason to obey rules that seem to change without reason. At home, norms exist, even in communities that are economically depressed. Therefore, when black children are faced with what seem to be normless situations in school, they rebel. "Somebody got to take charge," a black student said, trying to justify terrorizing his classmates and teachers.

4. *Isolation.* Feeling left out of most school events, many alienated black students become social isolates, developing few close friends among their classmates. Alienated students do not experience much success in school, and they do not believe that they are an integral part of school. Equally important, they have no control over relevant aspects of their educational process.

There are several ways students of all ethnic groups adjust to alienation. Some of them *retreat*—they withdraw and refuse to play the education game. Dropping out of school or getting hooked on drugs are ways of retreating. Other ways include tuning out teachers by daydreaming and doodling. Sometimes race combines with class discrimination to cause an alienated student to tune out. Consider, for example, the following classroom situation as illustration.

Mrs. K. was standing at her desk taking the class attendance roll. Two well-dressed, middle-class black girls entered the room, talking loudly. Without looking up, Mrs. K. said, "Michele and Faith, please take your seats and be quiet. The tardy bell has rung and you're late, but I won't report it. I hope you will tell me after class what was so interesting you couldn't get to class on time."

A few seconds later another black student entered the room. He was shabbily dressed and his hair was uncombed. Mrs. K. stopped taking attendance and looked up. "Didn't you hear the bell, Roland?," she said, frowning. "You know I'll have to mark you tardy and report you to the office. You act as though school rules don't apply to you."

Roland hunched his shoulders and continued walking until he reached his desk. He slid quietly into his seat, crumpling up his written excuse and dropping it on the floor, then began staring out the window.

Without trying to do so, Mrs. K. behaved in a highly discriminatory manner. A white student treated the same as Roland was would have probably behaved the same way. Either all three or none of the students should have been marked tardy. But before making that decision, Mrs. K. should have asked the students to explain their tardiness. If rules are to be fair, they must be fairly and consistently administered. And if students are to believe teachers are fair-minded, they must be treated fairly.

In other instances, black students aspire to succeed in school but either lack the requisite knowledge or do not believe they can do well in school by following the established procedures. These students *negatively innovate*—they use unacceptable means to succeed in school, such as cheating on examinations, stealing quizzes, and extorting help from high-achieving students. Few lower-class black students can get ahead by adhering to school rules and regulations. Middle-class black students can, but they seldom share their knowledge or coping skills with lower-class students.

Some black students seek only to get by without getting in trouble. School life becomes a *ritual* in which their only goal is good classroom behavior, to glide through school as easily and quickly as possible.

In rare instances, low-achieving black students get the help they need to *conform* to school requirements. Conformists attend remedial courses, receiving the attention they need from sensitive and well-prepared teachers. While relatively few in number, their impact is significant. They dispel the myth that low-achieving black students are doomed to failure. Instead, they frequently become the first in their family to graduate from high school or go to college.

As said before, students who fail in school are usually defensive. For example, black students who believe they are incapable of passing courses often deny the importance of school. "We don't need no diploma to make it. We can get some mules [people to sell narcotics] or hoes [whores] and make more money than the whole damn school full of teachers," a disappointed black male student told a friend when he looked at the failing grades on his report card. Oral recitations in the classroom also add to this feeling, causing them to feel stupid in front of their homies [friends]. In many instances, black students who do know the correct answer will refuse to volunteer it so as to avoid embarrassing low-achieving black students or becoming a "sellout." They are less magnanimous with low-achieving white students.

To put it bluntly, fewer and fewer black students are learning the basic skills. It is obvious that alienation, with all its unfortunate concomitants, is both a cause and a result of low achievement. Some stark conclusions can be drawn from these facts.

The successful programs that currently exist must be increased in number and scope merely to "hold the line" in preventing the creation of an even larger proportion of uneducated black youth. That is, intervention activities that work must be replicated to accommodate the increasing black student population.

There are those, both professional and nonprofessional, who advocate punishment and strict discipline or psychiatric treatment for alienated black students. These methods, though, are seldom effective. People who believe that punishment will stop deviant school behaviors should heed educators who state that punishment per se has never proved an effective deterrent. Nor is strict discipline a good solution. After all, alienated black children come from a variety of home situations, including those in which parents are overly strict, lax, or inconsistent in administering discipline. Reasonable guidance and understanding between teachers and students are more likely to produce conformity to school norms.

Psychiatric treatment is not a cure-all either. Nor do the vast majority of alienated black students need psychiatric help. Furthermore, therapy does not teach children how to behave or read—only to analyze their feelings about behaving badly or not reading. It appears that solutions to black students' alienation must focus on teacher behavior. Any intervention should take into account who the students are, the nature of their community life, and their educational needs. Since most low-achieving black students are hooked on failure, teachers must not be pushers or enablers—individuals who supply students with deadly doses of failure.

The Deprived Student Syndrome

Much of the plight of teachers (white and nonwhite) assigned to teach students who live in economically depressed rural and urban areas stems from their inability to understand the educational needs of culturally different people. Many teachers erroneously think that black students require only kindness, when what they really need is an education. With so much emphasis being placed on understanding and assisting minority-group students, some teachers, usually white, fall victim to the urge to engage in overcompensatory behavior. No matter how well intended, however, social promotion, a watered-down curriculum, and unearned rewards cause, not alleviate, problems. They may, in fact, lead to the *deprived student syndrome*, the process by which black students use their deprivations as an excuse for not doing schoolwork.

This is a tragic blend of guile and self-defeat, because it encourages some students to take pride in how few of the required class assignments they had to complete to pass a course. Obviously, the deprived student syndrome hurts students. Less obvious is its negative effect on the teaching profession. When informed of this game, a jaded teacher said, "It (the deception) doesn't hurt me. I've got my education. Those kids will never get theirs." Another teacher snarled, "Let them rot in their own ignorance." When teachers become willing partners in the process, they call into question the ethical standards of their profession.

"When I wants to get out of doing school assignments," a black high school student confided, "I just tells my white teachers that I couldn't do them because my old man was drunk, or the light company turned off the lights. I can't git ovah on black teachers, though." This is beating the system—getting by without doing the required work. Using their community circumstances as a crutch, these students hobble through school, manipulating the system. "If I wants to sack in late and miss my first class," says another black student, "I don't worry about it. My principal says it's a miracle that I come to school at all—with all the hardships that I have to put up with." Few students in this category are seeking success in school; they only seek to minimize the complications during their stay.

To the student who knows that he or she is not doing the required work but still receives positive feedback, success in school is meaningless and good grades are a farce. Many of these students have come to wish that their teachers had required more of them. Commenting on her school performance, a black high school graduate said, "I got through with no sweat, but it didn't learn me anything.... If I had to do it over again, I'd study harder. Now the only thing that I can do is low-pay work or something that don't call for an educated person." School under these conditions becomes a game in which the winners still lose— at school and, later, in the workplace.

Summary

Low-achieving students are more likely to conform to school rules and procedures if they believe that conformity is for their benefit and not the system's or the teacher's. All students, and particularly poor blacks, need teachers who will (1) be honest in evaluating their work, (2) tell them where they are in subject-matter skill development, and (3) assist them in their efforts to improve.

White teachers can change black students' attitudes toward learning by uncritically accepting questions and ideas (but not ignoring incorrect speech or unacceptable behavior) and by helping them develop sophisticated skills of inquiry, such as how to sustain, refine, and test a hypothesis. Furthermore, all students learn better in classes where they feel wanted and respected. Therefore, the classroom climate must take into account students' feelings; it should not be focused only on learning subject matter. Black students must first believe their teachers accept them as worthy beings before they can comfortably venture forth into ego-threatening classroom learning situations.

The characteristics of school programs that help black children form positive attitudes toward themselves, toward others, and toward learning can be outlined as follows. That program is most desirable which
1. accepts black students as they are, while helping them to master school subjects—especially reading, writing, and speaking.
2. helps black children understand the reasons why culturally different people behave as they do.

3. fosters interaction among different ethnic groups, with each being given equal status. Every child in every classroom is given an equal opportunity, within the limits of his or her ability, to experience genuine success in school tasks.
4. helps each student accomplish school assignments at the highest level possible but not at the expense of other students. Learning is best when all students can be winners.

Most important for poor black parents is the hope that their children can get a good education and become first-generation vocational-technical school or college graduates. Some of these children do graduate, get good jobs, and move into the middle class, and their offspring become the first generation out of poverty. Sometimes discouraged white teachers lament, "We only graduated a few black children who have done well as adults." But they do not understand the potential importance of those few. They do not know how much they have done to help save a family—or a community. Yes, teachers matter very much.

Chapter 6

Supervising
Black Workers

Work is a basic indicator of success in modern cultures; most people organize their lives around their occupations. Consequently, grave psychological disturbances can result when people who are able to work are unable to get a job. And when black Americans are unable to find or keep jobs because of racial discrimination, their ethnicity becomes a handicap (Kirschenman and Neckerman 1991). Most black Americans are unconvinced of the sincerity of white employers who say that they are not prejudiced and will gladly hire qualified blacks, because more blacks than whites who are qualified for jobs do not get them. Too often, the term *qualified* means "superqualified" when used with reference to black applicants. Even when they do manage to get a job, numerous black workers are confronted with additional barriers, mainly those pertaining to supervision.

The problems centering on supervising black workers are exacerbated when white employees must, for the first time, compete with blacks for high-level jobs. Even though they occupy nearly 90 percent of managerial positions, many white employees behave as though they are on the verge of losing their job entitlements. Thomas Kochman described these individuals, largely white males, as behaving "like the firstborn in the family, the ones who have

144 Our Souls to Keep

had the best of both parents and never forgave the second child for being born" (Galen and Palmer 1994, 52). Blacks are the "second-born children" in the workplace. The transition from a workplace dominated by white managers and supervisors to one where people of color are statistically prominent can be a national prescription for racial equality—or for disaster, because it is also fraught with tension and conflict.

Walking a tightrope, administrators who are responsible for resolving intergroup conflict must be able to give their black subordinates fair guidance and support without further alienating their white coworkers. It is a balancing act that produces numerous casualties. For example, if white managers seem to favor black workers, white workers secretly label these administrators "nigger lovers." If they seem to favor white workers, black workers call them "racists." Even so, equal employment opportunity in the workplace is not only morally right, it is required by law. Violation of an individual's civil rights makes the perpetrators as well as their organizations liable for actual and punitive damages. This is not "political correctness," it is good business. For people concerned about the "bottom line," it is very simple: racial discrimination hurts organizations and the nation. For example, the nation's economy loses hundreds of millions of dollars each year because of employment discrimination (Brimmer 1993).

A Vicious Circle

Individual and group employment practices based on unfounded racial myths have caused countless black workers to be relegated to dead-end jobs. These practices are great hurdles that black Americans have to surmount, because they are built on both actual and imagined impediments. Most black Americans strongly desire to be economically productive citizens; however, traditional attitudes toward them obstruct achievement of this goal.

Black workers are caught up in a kind of vicious circle from which few have been able to extricate themselves. It goes like this: (1) job opportunities are assigned according to social and economic status, in which whites have the advantage; (2) social mobility and the attainment of social and economic status are based primarily on jobs; (3) most blacks do not fare well when competing for jobs with whites and therefore have difficulty improving their status; and (4) they remain subordinate to whites with little hope of moving up. The net result is that black Americans are proportionally unemployed and underemployed compared to whites. There are many deluded white workers who believe that affirmative action programs have shifted most job opportunities to blacks and women, hence the charge of "reverse discrimination." This notion, however, is grounded in a lot of emotion and few facts.

There is a danger inherent in attributing the vicious circle exclusively to the pernicious nature of racism. Too much emphasis placed on racism and too little attention given to self-empowerment can immobilize blacks. Throughout American history black leaders have cautioned their followers to neither wallow in despair nor let the memory of slavery immobilize them. Blacks who are fixated on the past are unable to take advantage of the opportunities that do come their way.

Helping black workers escape the vicious circle is not merely the process of giving black employees more authority through job assignments. It also means fully utilizing their knowledge and skills while simultaneously preparing them for higher-level jobs. As they advance in the organization, black and white executives and managers need to become role models and mentors for other employees, black and white alike. But it is difficult to mentor blacks who are "hidden" in organizations.

Except for prominently displaying a few token blacks in high-profile positions, it is a common practice for business organizations to hide most black employees in positions that minimize their visibility. Thus blacks are more likely to be employed as inventory clerks than as receptionists. Black females who are assigned front-line jobs most often have Caucasian-like physical features, particularly in skin color and nose shape. In some workplaces such as hotels and motels, blacks are restricted to stereotypical jobs such as busboys, doormen, and maids. While few employers admit it, most of them place more emphasis on promoting "white-looking" blacks and less on promoting "black-looking" employees. For similar reasons, many organizations proudly display their "good-looking" black employees and hide the less attractive ones. When employers hire, place, and promote blacks based on ability and not skin color or physical features, a broad spectrum of blacks can be found in all positions in the organization.

Glass Ceiling

To the metaphor of the vicious circle discussed above must be added the metaphor of the glass ceiling. If women in the workplace are restrained from reaching top management positions by a glass ceiling, so are black employees. As noted above, black employees must be groomed or mentored for upper-echelon positions just as whites are. Without mentors they do not learn how to navigate the specific rules of protocol, dress, and demeanor of the workplace environment. A frustrated junior-level black executive said, "They [white senior executives] simply don't talk to me.... They won't let me in their inner circle where I can learn what to do to get ahead."

Ingroup culture in the workplace prevents a large number of blacks from feeling welcome in predominantly white organizations. Consequently, few blacks are defined by whites as "fitting in" the organizational culture. By denying them organizational knowledge, white managers and supervisors effectively curtail black workers' careers. It is common for black and white employees entering jobs at the same time to move at different speeds and along different paths. A few years later, the white workers will tend to have higher salaries and will have received more promotions. Considerably fewer black employees are on the fast track of success; most of them are in stagnant ruts leading at best to lateral job transfers. Consequently, most black employees have *jobs* while their white counterparts have *careers*.

Blacks who manage to attain managerial or executive status in corporate America are often employed in such staff positions as affirmative action officers or community affairs managers. Others are assistants to administrators. These individuals usually have small staffs and little direct control over corporate budgets or production. Few white CEOs are willing to risk appointing blacks to important administrative line positions, unlike fast-track white employees, who are given line assignments in which they control large budgets, numerous employees, and substantial production processes. And the few blacks in such positions are seldom encouraged to mentor other blacks. Instead, they are expected to mentor promising white employees. With relatively few mentors—black or white—in most organizations, it is not surprising that most blacks are stuck in dead-end jobs, unable to break through the glass ceiling.

The most important activities of a mentor consist of allowing black workers time to talk about themselves and to learn about the environment in which they work, the tasks they are expected to do, and job and professional development opportunities. During this interaction, mentors should not tell black workers, "Don't be embarrassed or feel guilty because you don't fully understand job requirements or procedures." They *are* embarrassed and they *do* feel guilty about this. Mentioning it only adds to their discomfort. Mentors should instead focus on the technical and political aspects of the job.

Blacks who manage to make it to the top of the hierarchy are frequently suspected of being less deserving than their white peers and are charged with being "affirmative action hires." Those who through their talents manage to dispel this charge are usually relegated to the category of "exceptional" (superblacks) and are often described by their white supervisors and subordinates as "black managers." White executives in comparable positions, however, are seldom referred to as "white managers." Employees should be identified by race, color, gender, or national origin only when there is a good business-related reason, for example, as part of an equal opportunity report. Otherwise, it is inappropriate.

It is rare for a black employee not to encounter his or her ethnicity as a barrier. A disgruntled black salesman said,

> Mediocre white guys get promoted, while the best and the brightest blacks get passed over. The few blacks who have even been considered for promotion were head and shoulders above the white guys who got the jobs. They [white managers] got their jobs by sucking up to the boss on the golf course or at the country club that doesn't accept blacks. If the superblacks can't make it to the top, I know there's no chance for the rest of us.

If this were an isolated allegation of racial inequality in the workplace, it could be dismissed as a rationalization used by a black employee who did not deserve consideration for promotion. But it is not an isolated case; many black workers tell similar stories.

The possible demise of mandated affirmative action programs bodes no good for blacks. In the words of a black labor union member, "The foxes [prejudiced white administrators] would be given responsibility for the welfare of the chickens [ethnic minorities].... A lot of chickens gonna be lost." On the positive side, blacks employed in predominantly white organizations might not be hindered by the stigma of being considered affirmative action hires. However, if the decline of affirmative action means fewer blacks will gain admission to college, there will probably be fewer blacks to worry about being called affirmative action hires. The number of blacks admitted to medical, dental, business, law, and engineering programs would probably be drastically reduced.

Most black workers, conditioned by the discriminatory job market, are suspicious of employers who encourage them to apply for jobs which will facilitate their upward mobility. They have heard of numerous instances in which employers went through the motions of advertising job openings and conducting interviews but then hired a preselected white applicant. This is a common practice in universities and businesses, and although also true for whites and other ethnic groups, disproportionately more blacks than whites are victimized by this process. If black workers are to risk seeking higher-level job opportunities, they need to be given fair interviews. "Particular white applicants are wired in [promised the jobs] before any ads are bought," a white personnel officer disclosed to a U.S. Office of Equal Employment Opportunity investigator. In the race with whites for jobs, a disproportionate number of blacks come in second, or not at all.

Problems in Leadership

It is extremely important that individuals in authority minimize unfair treatment and maximize fair treatment within their spheres of influence. For example, when white employees observe white supervisors continuously rejecting and downgrading black employees, they believe that to be acceptable behavior, so they too reject and downgrade black employees. White administrators who fail to practice responsible leadership can aggravate racial bickering and even open hostility in the workplace. When racial discrimination in the workplace is applied consistently and continuously, black workers engage in self-deprecatory behaviors and are oppressed by feelings of inferiority. If these workplace problems are not resolved expeditiously and in an equitable manner, the organizational climate becomes intractably hostile.

Because of the way they look, talk, or behave, some black employees frustrate or irritate white managers and supervisors. Blacks who do not fit the highly subjective characteristics of "good workers" are usually labeled as "undesirable" or "problems." When these workers get in trouble, white administrators are not empathetic or forgiving. Fortunately, an increasing number of white administrators are coming to terms with their own racism and that of their colleagues. The information in the remainder of this section is a compilation of relevant attitudes, beliefs, values, and behaviors that can create either a smoothly functioning interracial organization or one where discrimination holds sway.

Errors in Leadership

White supervisors most frequently make three types of errors when interacting with black subordinates. The first is to promote the *illusion of color blindness*, whereby blacks are viewed as being just like whites. As a whole, black Americans dislike being told by white people, "I don't see you as a black person. I think of you as being just like me." This illusion downplays unique racial or ethnic experiences that characterize tradition-oriented blacks. There are many instances when race or ethnicity does matter. Not to see a black person as black is not to see an individual who may be denied promotion opportunities solely because of his or her race, a person who may be perceived by some white employees as being racially inferior.

The second error is the opposite of the illusion of color blindness: the assumption of the *irreversible mark of blackness*, the false assumption that all problems involving black American workers are about race. There are many times when race does not matter, for example, problems caused by inadequate job skills. A black entry-level supervisor told his white boss, "I'm grateful that you are sensitive to race relations problems and want to talk about them, but I need to talk first about the computer areas I'm deficient in." The third error is the *great white father/mother syndrome*. This view places whites in the role of saviors of blacks. These white managers and supervisors are comfortable when helping or managing blacks; they are uncomfortable being helped or supervised *by* blacks. In essence, their paternalism stifles black workers. In most instances, this kind of treatment by management is unconscious, but intentional or unintentional, black workers are the victims. "My manager thinks that she's my keeper—like in some kind of biblical injunction," a black clerk said in a job discrimination deposition. "I don't need to be kept, I need to be treated like an adult, like she treats the white clerks."

Three Styles of Leadership

Some white supervisors avoid contact with black subordinates as much as possible. They are *laissez-faire leaders*, individuals who project little confidence in their ability to supervise blacks. They spend a considerable amount of time away from their black subordinates, giving them too much responsibility and too little guidance. Predictably, their subordinates have low morale and marginal or inadequate productivity. Frustration, insecurity, and failure among black workers with such supervisors are extensive. Without active leadership there are no meaningful work goals around which they can coalesce. If left unchecked, the frustrations growing out of the situation will lead to indifference or resignations. To make matters worse, often these same supervisors are quite direct and interactive with their white (especially male) subordinates, perpetuating a white "good old boys club."

Other white supervisors of black workers are *autocratic leaders*, strict disciplinarians who tend to delegate very little decision-making responsibility to black members of the team. They make themselves the primary source of all production standards for black workers but give the white workers more leeway. Though autocratic leaders may get a considerable amount of work from their black subordinates, loyalty and employee initiative are not forthcoming. A black draftsman said, "Anybody can follow orders but they do it with more dedication when they are treated like valued employees."

Democratic leaders share with all subordinates the responsibility for planning and carrying out job mandates. They explain the whys of specific activities, rules, and procedures to all subordinates. And they seldom deliver praise or criticism in personal terms but rather in terms of work goals and results. With or without the supervisor present, black workers who are members of democratically led groups display high morale and achieve a high level of intergroup cooperation. This is the best situation for any employee to be in.

Studies of leadership clearly illustrate that there is no single list of traits characterizing effective managers and supervisors; nonetheless, some attributes are frequently cited: (1) the ability to speak and write fluently, (2) an inner drive to succeed, (3) the capacity to take responsibility and the initiative to seek it out, (4) the ability to get others to cooperate, (5) tact and courtesy, and (6) the ability to plan and organize the work of others. Effective managers and supervisors are able to get their employees to identify with the organization's work goals and to help them reach those goals. Job identification occurs when a worker adopts the values, interests, and approved behaviors of the organization. All employees achieve maximum job proficiency only when they have been inspired to do so.

It is extremely important for supervisors to remember that each employee is an individual first and should not be placed in an ethnic or racial category. Each must be encouraged to develop to the limit of his or her capacity, but for all employees, more than encouragement is needed. Opportunities must also be provided.

Types of Black Workers

An astute white CEO once observed that all workers in general and black workers in particular in his organization could be grouped into four categories which exhibit the following traits: hostility, dependence, independence, and cooperativeness.

Hostile black workers come to the workplace angry about racial oppression—real and imagined; they resent white authority. These individuals must be dealt with firmly but fairly in order to confine their aggressiveness and channel their energies toward the organization's objectives. Some black workers become hostile when they believe that their white supervisors and coworkers define them as affirmative action hires. Supervisors sometimes mistakenly assume that the negative attitudes of these workers are always groundless. They may in fact be well grounded in specific instances of discriminatory treatment. Most black workers who publicly challenge their supervisors earn little but scorn from their bosses, who label them "troublemakers."

Dependent black workers also need firm guidance, but for a different reason. They often enter the workplace conditioned by previous failures to believe that they are less skilled or intellectually inferior to most white people. Without supervision and support these workers will flounder. Black workers with low self-esteem tend to defer to their white coworkers' opinions on how best to do their jobs. Few organizations are prepared to provide the amount of supervision that extremely dependent employees of any ethnic group may need, a need that is magnified when the employees are black and self-deprecatory or resentful. "I can't do anything right," a black worker said, "and the white guys can't do anything wrong."

Individualists, or lone wolves, work best when left alone. However, supervisors should make sure that these independent employees are on course and not working at cross-purposes with the organization. With proper supervision individualists are good fast-track candidates. Few tradition-oriented black workers, however, are in this category; most tend not to feel comfortable working alone.

Cooperative black workers function best on a team where they have the opportunity to participate fully in decision making. They can usually operate within set policies, and they need little guidance or control. These employees are also good fast-track candidates. The trend in some organizations away from an emphasis on individual competition to one on teamwork is consonant with traditional African American collectivist values. Within such an organizational culture, black workers do not merely survive, they thrive.

Comfort Zones

Most white Americans perceive black men as threatening; the stereotype of the dangerous black man is widespread. Whites who accuse black males of robbery, kidnapping, or murder are more readily believed by law enforcement officials and community residents than are blacks who accuse white males of similar crimes. The racist presumption is that black males are criminals by nature and have a propensity for violence. Some white workers internalize these stereotypes to the degree that they become panic-stricken when they are alone in a room or an elevator with a black man (sensing the discomfort of these persons, mischievous black males may deliberately move closer to them or merely stare).

Stereotypes achieve some of their credibility because there are kernels of truth in them. There are times when blacks are physically aggressive, poorly prepared for certain jobs, and undependable. But this is equally true of individuals in all ethnic groups. An insidious aspect of these stereotypes is that some blacks believe them also. A prominent black civil rights leader told an audience that he too becomes fearful when approached in an isolated place by an unknown black male. "For some reason, I am not afraid if the guy is white," he confided. The fear of violence is not without basis (Chambers 1995; Free 1993; Whitaker 1990). It is a sad commentary that there are more black males in prison than in college. A white social worker in Montgomery, Alabama, said, "We [people in her agency] used to worry about how to protect blacks from the Ku Klux Klan. Now we worry about how to protect ourselves from [black male] clients." (In reality, most white Americans have little to fear from black Americans. Almost all black homicides, for example, occur in the black community.) The fear of black males frequently shows up in the workplace. The supervisor in the following exchange understood this fear but was uncowed by it.

Mrs. M. assigned her subordinates to teams of four to find ways to solve particular production problems. The next day, Sally, a slightly built white employee, asked to be reassigned to another team. Mrs. M. asked for reasons and Sally gave several, each of which Mrs. M. considered inadequate. Finally, Sally said in a low voice, "There are two black men in my group, and my husband said that I can't socialize with them."

Mrs. M. looked knowingly at Sally and answered in a soft voice, "Tell your husband that I'm not requiring you to socialize with them, only to work with them."

Fear of black coworkers escalates when whites encounter blacks (or other ethnic minorities) in groups. "They shouldn't segregate themselves," a white supervisor complained. "If they want to be like all other Americans, they should stop clustering." He was not concerned that there were all-white groups at the plant. In fact, blacks made up less than 2 percent of the workforce. In this instance the blacks had merely formed an all-black lunch group. When a white friend told of the concern, a black worker replied, "There are far more of you than of us. Hell, what do you think we're doing at lunch, planning how to seize control of the plant?" The pressure of being a minority-group worker can cause intense hostility and emotional distress. A few minutes at lunch or during a break with other black workers can provide the emotional nourishment some individuals need to carry out their jobs.

Black workers may be rejected by white supervisors for various reasons. Socially undesirable black workers are perceived as crude. Attitudinally undesirable black workers are accused of being ungrateful, arrogant, or uppity. Physically undesirable black workers are avoided because they have physical features that deviate greatly from white norms. Circumstantially undesirable black workers, because of diversity initiatives, are hired into positions previously held by white workers and may become chance targets of rejection.

The Skills Managers Need

Some organizations resemble nations at war. Workers who are verbally abused and discriminated against often become alcoholics, develop ulcers or mental problems, or burn out. Black employees in such organizations desperately need to be at peace both with the organization and with themselves. No organization should be a racial battlefield. Needless to say, if this situation is to be abated, the best possible managers and supervisors are required. Aggrieved black workers must be given the chance to resolve their problems through humane diversity management—by nurturing black employees and preserving the dignity of those who are to be terminated. Considerable human relations skills are needed to perform these tasks, skills Mr. White, as seen in the next illustration, certainly lacked.

> Mr. White, the supervisor, called a meeting for all the employees in his section. He was extremely irate because of unacceptable behavior that he had observed over the past three weeks. The black employees became noticeably uncomfortable as Mr. White focused his criticism on them.

Mr. White: I've called this meeting today to discuss some behaviors that are completely unacceptable. You people are not supporting this company. You aren't following the rules! Brown, you've been late at least one day each week for the last three weeks. Thomas, I've seen you out of uniform several times, and you're not the only one who does this. And I've noticed that a lot of you are taking breaks outside the break area. This is ridiculous. I'm not going to take much more of it. I hired you and I can fire you. All that I ask is you give us a good day's work for a good day's pay. You people need to abide by the rules! Don't make me fire you. Why can't you fit in like Ruby Jones? Now are we all clear on this?

Mr. Brown: I would like to explain why I was late. I've been taking classes at the university and sometimes I get caught in traffic. It seems to me you don't care that some of us are trying to prepare for better jobs in this company.

Mr. White: Obviously we care. We gave you a job so you can have the means to support your family, didn't we? However, it's important that you get your priorities straight. And your first priority is to get to work on time.

Mr. Thomas: I have a question. Why do we have to wear these uniforms? They cost a lot of money and we have to buy them out of our pocket. Some of us have been out of uniform because ours are worn out and we have to save up money to buy new ones.

Mr. White: I understand that they cost money, but that's just part of the job. You knew that when you were hired. The policy hasn't changed.

Mr. Thomas: One more question. Why do we have to go to the break area to take a break? The supervisors take theirs anywhere they want to.

Mr. White: You shouldn't concern yourself with that. That's just company policy, and I expect you to follow company policy. Now I hope these problems are going to be solved. Let's get back to work.

Mr. White certainly should not have referred to the black

employees as "you people." In doing so, he not only used a demeaning term but also set up an "us-them" dichotomy. As for the break policy, he could have told them that he would ask management to reconsider it. Even if the policy were not reversed, White's bringing the request to higher-ups would have demonstrated respect and concern for the employees. Comparing one employee (Ruby Jones) with others further alienated the black employees because of their cultural norms—family or group members avoid doing things that embarrass each other. Also, Mr. White should have commended Mr. Brown for continuing his education. Further, if company policy permitted, Mr. Brown should have been offered options regarding his inability to always arrive at work on time, for example, work later, take shorter breaks, or consider occasional lateness as an excused absence. If the uniforms were important, the company could have provided an allowance for them or had a reasonable grace period for employees to purchase them. In summary, the supervisor should have made an effort to help the employees comply with and/or change some of the company policies, not just stonewall their objections.

Sometimes racially insensitive supervisors have difficulty acknowledging their own shortcomings.

> Henry was not in a good mood when he finished reading a confidential letter from his boss, Paul. Damn vice presidents spend too much time micromanaging and not enough time doing their jobs, Henry thought as he shredded the letter. However, nothing, not even destroying the letter, would help him forget its contents. These words were indelibly lodged in his mind: "You have been found guilty of racially insensitive behavior that borders on discrimination. In accordance with the steps outlined below, you will cease this behavior. Furthermore, you will attend next month's corporate cultural diversity training seminar...." "Bullshit," Henry said out loud.
>
> At that moment Chris, an African American man-

ager in Henry's department, came to the door. "Got a minute?" Chris asked, trying to pretend that he had not overheard Henry's outburst.

"Sure, guy," Henry answered. "Come in. What can I do for you?" He was never quite comfortable around Chris—or any other black employees.

"It's about the inventory...," Chris began.

Henry cut him off. "How about those Lions? Give me eight black studs like those Lions have on offense and I'll beat the Vikings any day. You lived in Detroit for a while, didn't you, guy?"

"Yes, but...." Chris could barely hear himself above Henry's small talk.

"Do you know any of those studs who play for the Lions?"

"About the inventory...," Chris began again.

"To hell with the inventory," Henry snarled, pulling nervously on his tie. "I need your advice about something."

Chris stared at Henry. This was going to be another of those "tell me about black jocks and any other black persons" conversation, he thought. He frowned, swallowed hard, and nodded.

"Do you think I engage in racially inappropriate behavior, Chris? I treat you okay, don't I? If all of the black people who work here were half as competent as you, I wouldn't get on their asses. I'm not a bigot. I eat soul food with you, I don't tell race jokes, and I don't complain about being passed over for promotion because Martin, who we both know is a bootlicking lackey of the vice president, got the job," Henry began. He looked at Chris for affirmation. "Am I?"

"Are you what?" Chris looked away.

"Am I a bigot?" Henry moved to position himself in line with Chris's stare.

There was a long silence.

"You could probably benefit from some race relations training, Henry," Chris said in his calmest voice.

"Bullshit," Henry replied. He walked out of his office, leaving Chris alone.

For some white supervisors like Henry, insight regarding their feelings about ethnic minorities and their behavior toward them is improved only during some type of cultural awareness training. Henry was indeed a prime candidate for such training. He believed himself to be a good guy in race relations. If racism were an addiction, Henry would have been diagnosed by clinicians as being in denial. Fortunately, during the mandated cultural diversity training, he was able to understand and learn how to apply the following common sense suggestions for effectively supervising black workers.

1. If black workers perceive the job climate differently from you, thank them for calling it to your attention. This does not commit either party to altering his or her own behavior. It does, however, help you objectively consider things from the other person's point of view.

2. Avoid the fallacies of the superblack theory, which defines high-achieving black workers as exceptional people who are better than lower-achieving black workers. They are more motivated or skilled in specific tasks, not better people.

3. If it is not common to call white employees by their first name, do not do so with black employees. Don't, for example, refer to a white worker as Ms. Smith and her black peer as Sally.

4. Avoid clichés and platitudes such as "One of my best friends is black" or "I went to school with blacks." The proof of your understanding of black workers will come from what you do when interacting with them, not your tales about black friends or classmates.

5. Do not tell black workers that they should consider themselves lucky to be in the organization. If they are qualified, the major determinant of their employment should be job skills, not luck. (As stated in earlier chap-

ters, many black workers probably doubt their ability to compete successfully with whites.) Give them assurance that they belong, not suspicion that they are unqualified or tokens.

6. Do not assume that a black employee is friendly with all the other black employees. They might share only their race.
7. Avoid offensive phraseology when addressing black workers. Terms such as "you people" and "your people" tend to create racial barriers where none may have been intended.
8. Do not expect black workers to behave like others you knew in the past. They may—or they may not.

In order to be effective, cultural awareness training programs must also be responsive to the perceptions of white employees. Henry's training was helpful in this respect: the trainers were composed of whites and ethnic minorities; all employees completed the training; the trainees were not publicly embarrassed by being forced to divulge their own feelings or behaviors; and the training was workplace-oriented, not personality-oriented. Once he became more insightful, Henry was able to accurately describe the level of his black subordinates' job skills or knowledge and to help them to improve. Consequently, he prepared them to cooperate or compete—whatever was required to get the job done.

Constructive and Destructive Pressure

Black employees cannot—and should not—escape from all pressure. A certain amount of pressure acts as a driving force, kindling the desire to finish a job, to go on to the next step. But there are differences between constructive and destructive pressure. Constructive pressure is closely tied to two other aspects of learning: motivation and the reward of satisfaction through achievement. Too much pressure is likely to result only in producing an attitude of distress and defeat. If supervisors are to help their black subordinates cope with workplace pressures, they must understand what those pressures are and develop effective methods to help blacks manage them. One of those pressures is competition.

The danger in allowing competition to provide the sole basis for success in organizations is becoming increasingly clear to workplace observers. Yet it is characteristic of U.S. organizations that employees are expected to move up the economic ladder through competitive individualism and the fear that if they cannot keep up with their peers they will be labeled failures. Blacks frequently decide that they do not want to get ahead if it will cost them their workplace friends and relationships both in the organization and back home. This is especially true when the culture of the organization requires blacks to talk, dress, and otherwise behave in ways that are believed by them to sell out their blackness for "white" success. They become workplace dropouts.

Pressure applied to achieve conformity will almost always backfire or fail. Supervisors who nag black workers to do better without understanding why they are underperforming will end up with even lower achievers. Pressure is positive only when it also arouses curiosity and interest and causes black workers to exert pressure from within themselves. Success stemming from inner pressure is much more effective and infinitely more rewarding to all Americans.

Negative job pressure in the form of shame is often used carelessly or indiscriminately, particularly with blacks—a look of disappointment, sarcastic and undermining remarks, and comparison of black workers with their high-achieving "brothers," "sisters," or peers. Instead of generating a higher quality of work, however, this approach tends to lower black employees' faith in themselves as well as in their supervisors. If managers want black subordinates to be creative, external pressure is seldom effective. Creativity develops from within, from the reservoir of ideas that flow out of the mind and demand recognition. Supervisors can create an atmosphere which fosters creativity, but they cannot create the ideas. As illustrated in the situation cited below, black workers who feel comfortable with their coworkers—who find it safe to ask questions, express ideas, and try new things even though they make mistakes—will be most responsive to pressure from within themselves.

> Supervisor: Jim, I noticed that you haven't said anything. I need as many ideas as I can get from this team before I go to the executive staff meeting next week.
>
> Jim: The other guys covered everything I would have said.
>
> Supervisor: Maybe they did or maybe they didn't. You have a way of giving designs a slightly different twist. Of course, the final design will be a team product—one we all agree on. We're not at that stage yet, but I need your ideas as well as Reginald's, Horace's, and Frank's.
>
> Jim: We're a team, Mike. I'll help them with the final design.
>
> Supervisor: Are you saying there's nothing you can add to their ideas that would give us an edge when I go to the meeting?
>
> Jim: Maybe there are a couple of things I can add. Give me another day. I'll take a closer look.

The next day Jim presented four ideas for the new design. His supervisor and coworkers commended him for coming up with "Jim's twist" to the project.

Cooperation and Competition

Techniques for developing a friendly, cooperative climate in organizations are so little understood by most managers and supervisors that they are used less frequently than techniques that foster competition. Competition, say these managers, is simply human nature. Actually, in cultures with a more collectivist orientation, including traditional black cultures, cooperation rather than competition is considered natural. Also, recent research suggests that, given the proper conditions, blacks and whites are as responsive to friendliness and goodwill as they are to conflict and hostility, as capable of cooperating as they are of competing.

As often happens—for example, a team project developed by a supervisor to help culturally diverse employees learn to work together—cooperation degenerates into intense competition for prestige positions on the team or for individual recognition of contributions to the work of the team. The desire to develop a cooperative work environment is not enough; managers and supervisors must put conscious effort into learning the techniques needed to make cooperation a reality. This involves, among other things,

1. accepting each employee and requiring reciprocal behavior among team members,
2. fostering interaction among employees in job-related activities conducted away from the workplace, such as conferences or retreats,
3. making it possible for each employee to achieve rewards but not at the expense of one's coworkers, and
4. encouraging employees to say "we" and "us" instead of "I" when describing team activities.

The emphasis on developing a cooperative social climate in the workplace should in no way preclude or diminish opportunities for individual growth. It is true that some black workers will compete with each other in various ways regardless of what supervisors do to encourage cooperation. It is also true that success in organizations requires constructive competition as well as cooperation. Both can be productive. Constructive competition among black workers centers on individual creativity ("doing one's own thing" or coming up with "Jim's twist" in a way that enhances the team's performance). Their "tell me what to do, but not how to do it" attitude is seen in athletic competition—creative moves and flamboyant responses to scoring. Always, however, the overarching objective, in sports or in the workplace, is for the team to win. The team is more important than any individual. It's like the old saying in the black community: "One monkey don't stop no show."

Roads to Success—or Failure

Black workers who believe themselves to be of the lowest social status perceive the workplace as grossly unfair. It is difficult if not impossible for them to believe in their personal competence when they are considered undesirable by their supervisors and coworkers. This situation facilitates failure, not success. Some supervisors expect black workers to fail, and if black workers share that expectation, they usually compete poorly for promotions. Believing that their failures are predetermined, they fall further and further behind their white peers in terms of career advances and become progressively more negative in discussions about job-related matters. If they decide that their emotional and physical well-being depends on minimizing the importance of occupational success, black employees will withdraw altogether from competition for better-paying jobs.

Even when white supervisors offer opportunities for advancement, black employees often question the intentions or motives of whites with whom they interact. They look beyond words and deeds to see if there is something that will further oppress them. The plant incident described below illustrates this point.

    White Plant Manager: Bill, I'd like to see you for a minute. [You'll be pleased with the news.]

    Bill: Sure. What's up? [Now what's wrong?]

    Plant Manager: You have done a fantastic job since I hired you. Your work habits sure proved to a lot of people that our affirmative action program works. [I'm glad we have good black employees.]

Bill: I've just tried to do my job, boss. [Here we go with some more affirmative action crap.]
Plant Manager: I'm going to recommend that you be promoted to supervisor of the midnight shift.
Bill: That's great news. [Hell, that's the worst shift in this plant. He's setting me up to fail.]
Plant Manager: You're the best person for the job. If there's anything I can do to help you after you start the new job, let me know. [Together we'll make sure that you succeed.]
Bill: I'll hold you to your offer. I'm sure that you'll be a valuable resource. [Hell will freeze over before I call you. I ain't going out like that. If I fail it won't be with your help. I'll be watching my back.]

Many blacks, like Bill, are conditioned by stories of friends "set up" to fail and leery of white offers to help. In addition, not wanting to let white people know that he has problems with assignments would prevent Bill from going to the plant manager for help. In this instance, the plant manager should follow through with his offer to help. As described in the case of Mike and his mentor, he must be proactive rather than reactive. He could tactfully query Bill about his progress: "When I had the job you've got, I made a lot of mistakes. Fortunately, my boss caught them before I messed up too much. I probably made every mistake in the book while I was learning the job. How are things going with you? How can I help you?"

Studies conclude that a major difference between white and black Americans is not their *ideal* occupational aspirations but their *real* aspirations. While workers of both groups have high ideals, most white employees expect to succeed in the workplace; most black employees do not and know that, even if they do, only a few will be allowed to move up to higher-level jobs. The mere fact that blacks see other blacks who have succeeded does not necessarily cause them to believe in themselves. For concerned whites, the key to successful intervention is to be patient and reassuring to otherwise competent blacks who are underachieving but hesitant to try taking advantage of opportunities to improve their situation. Failure is easy. They have done it. Success is more problematic. Blacks fear success. They fear that if they succeed, they may fail soon afterward.

One of the more significant conclusions found in the hundreds of studies focusing on the self-esteem of black workers is the need for organizations to develop procedures to assist low achievers adjust to their work environment. The potpourri of hopes, fears, and behaviors that blacks bring with them to their jobs is shaped in the community. To be successful on the job, black workers need help in adjusting to workplace requirements.

White supervisors can help black employees in performance reviews and/or through career counseling. If done well, this process encourages black employees to talk about their job deficiencies and, where necessary, seek appropriate training. During this process, it is imperative for white supervisors to divert black employees from wallowing in self-pity. "Poor black me" and "I'll never be able to learn this" attitudes are counterproductive. Specifically, there are four suggestions white supervisors can follow to enculturate and empower black employees: (1) involve them in on-the-job-training, (2) send them to formal training programs that provide a series of planned job-related experiences, (3) provide formal sponsors or mentors, and (4) encourage them to participate in job-related conferences. Blacks are typically excluded from these things.

It is inadvisable for organizations to run training programs designed solely for blacks or other minorities. White employees (and many blacks) will see them as "dummy training." It also elicits from white employees charges of "tokenism" and "reverse discrimination," and sometimes unintentionally reinforces stereotypes about inferior black workers. Instead, blacks should be given opportunities to be involved in organization-wide activities that can enhance their job skills, integrate them into the organization, and bolster their self-image. Whatever training is utilized, supervisors should not make unsubstantiated assumptions about what black workers can and cannot do; they must be given a fair chance to succeed. A black factory worker's experience illustrates this point.

> I was never given a chance to change jobs. In fact, I was not even in the final pool of a supervisory job that I was qualified for. Nothing in my folder mentions the vo-tech courses I completed. There is no mention of my military training. When I asked why these documents weren't included in my file, the personnel director said that I had not provided official verification. He had never asked me for official verification—just like he didn't for the white guy who was promoted based on things they said he had done that qualified him for the promotion.

The sense of being a successful employee comes from task mastery, recognition for work done well, and a positive self-image. In order for managers and supervisors to facilitate optimum career development for their subordinates, especially those who are among the most difficult personalities to manage or supervise effectively, they must understand each subordinate's range of abilities and style of learning. Then they must build on the skills of each individual. If successful, this process will help their subordinates shift negative self-images to positive ones. Four things must occur for this to happen.

First, supervisors must give more than lip service to fostering self-direction in workers. The disproportionately small number of black workers who are described by their supervisors as being self-directed indicates a need for improvement in this area. Supervisors must believe that self-direction in blacks is important. Also, supervisors must find out what blacks want to achieve in their jobs.

Second, supervisors must learn to trust black workers to be capable of carrying out new assignments. Too often white supervisors paternalistically try to protect black workers from failure and consequently do not give them new or challenging assignments. It is not unusual for black workers, more so than for their white counterparts, to describe themselves as being bored or unchallenged by their jobs. That is, after mastering the rudiments, they spend most of their time doing repetitive tasks. Responsibility, a positive self-image, and self-direction are learned through meaningful tasks and new challenges.

Third, effective supervisors maintain an experimental attitude. They are not surprised when black or any other workers with a low self-image fail to carry out new assignments. Nor do these supervisors assume an "I told you so" attitude. People fearful of making mistakes will be hesitant to try new assignments. Black workers are also typically uneasy about being assigned to jobs previously filled by white employees. They fear "letting other black people down" by failing; they fear being set up by supervisors to fail; they fear failure itself. This attitude stands squarely in the way of black employees doing their best work. People fearful of making mistakes will not risk trying, and if they won't try, they will never feel encouraged to discover their own self-direction and creativity.

Fourth, previously unemployed and underemployed workers must be encouraged not only to excel but to learn to feel comfortable with success. Because of societal conditioning, black workers tend to question their good fortune and to feel leery of it (white workers tend to wonder why they did not succeed sooner). Black workers who believe in their supervisors and feel comfortable with them have less difficulty learning to excel and accepting their achievements than do those who have hostile supervisors.

In summary, supervisors should not give up hope when black employees falter or fail. Problems involving self-direction and low levels of confidence are not amenable to quick and easy solutions. However, the following "dos and don'ts" may be helpful for managers and supervisors. Although these tips focus on blacks, they are applicable to all employees.

Managers and supervisors should

1. *have and be able to convey genuine sensitivity for the concerns of black workers.* These concerns may include (a) being torn by the divergence between job performance and the expectations of their relatives and friends, (b) lack of experience working with whites as equals, (c) inadequate promotion opportunities, and (d) occupational pigeonholing;

2. *have an understanding of how black community norms can affect workplace activities.* Black workers frequently bring to the workplace community beliefs, values, and attitudes that negatively affect their job performance;

3. *get to know individual black workers and convey to each of them in a noncondescending way that you are sensitive to their needs and concerns.* Managers and supervisors must make a special effort to establish rapport with black workers and convey their desire to assist in problem solving and job enhancement;

4. *be fair and ensure that all employees know and understand the organization's standards, policies, and procedures.* Black workers in particular need to know that they have the right to succeed or fail based on their job performance, not because of their race;

5. *listen carefully for negative and positive feelings.* Feed back this information; seek clarity and understanding. Build on positive feelings and try through supportive actions to defuse negative ones; and

6. *recognize the limits of one's authority and expertise.* Know when it is appropriate to refer black workers to someone else or some agency with more specialization in abating race-centered problems.

Managers and supervisors should not

1. make unsubstantiated assumptions about blacks and what jobs they can and cannot do;

2. argue with or admonish blacks who need counseling. This will cause them to become defensive, and they will not share their feelings;

3. flaunt authority (organizational or intellectual). Talk *with* them, not at them; and
4. give unsolicited advice on racial issues. If they ask for advice, encourage black workers to consider how particular beliefs and behaviors may facilitate or impede their job performance. Allow them to pursue options that will improve their performance or enhance their careers.

Demeaning Language—Not a Laughing Matter

Aggressive language is a major problem in the workplace. Many white employees fear people who are culturally different from them, as this old saying poignantly reminds us:

> What people do not know, they tend to fear; what they fear, they distrust; what they distrust, they will try to avoid; what they distrust and cannot avoid, they will try to change to fit their concept of "normality"; what they cannot change, they will try to isolate or destroy.

Many white workers feel this way about black workers whom they do not know. A subtle way of destroying black workers is through aggressive discourse, which erroneously appears to be less harmful than physical aggression.

Though the consequences of hateful words differ from physical violence, they are no less painful. For example, white supervisors who use epithets to describe blacks are not just using words; the effect of the epithets is very real, the emotional consequences, extremely negative, since they are, in effect, verbal oppression. Ultimately, such language filters throughout the organization and triggers behavior consistent with the epithets. The fact that "niggers," for example, are not hired in some organizations, are fired in others, and not promoted in still others is concrete evidence of the power of verbal abuse.

Anything that verbally or in written form demeans employees is destructive. Whether spoken, transmitted through memoranda or e-mail, or scribbled on desks or lockers, these communications create a hostile work environment. While many of these behaviors may not be punishable by law, they indicate intolerance and are hurtful. An African American in one organization took a day off to celebrate Martin Luther King Jr. Day. Upon returning to work, he received this anonymous e-mail message: "If I kill one more nigger, you people will get another day off."

Even more pervasive than overt racist comments is symbolic racism. Whereas racial slurs, epithets, and graffiti are clearly racist in their tone, most of today's workplace hate communication is more subtle. Few bigoted supervisors publicly utter racial slurs. Instead, they vent their verbal venom through "innocent'" stories, such as telling about a black man's insatiable sexual appetite or a black jock's athletic prowess (like Henry, earlier in this chapter). The objective of the story is, through implication, to impute a negative characteristic to blacks or to stereotype them. More often than not, when challenged, the storyteller will say something like "I have nothing against them.... Some of my best friends are black." Some of these "innocent" messages are nonverbal, such as giving a black employee a watermelon with candles on it as a birthday "cake." If called to task about this racist gesture, the "joker" will quip, "Aw, come on, can't you take a joke?" The fact is, however, that blacks are defamed or depersonalized.

Calling people's attention to the offensive nature of what they assumed was an innocent, funny story or joke can bring them up short. If they offer the excuse, "It's only a story," you can counter with "It may only be a story to you, but it is not funny to those at whose expense it is told." Nor should you accept as adequate the explanation "I didn't mean any harm" or "I was only joking." No harm may have been intended, but the result is harmful.

The issue of whether or not to intervene when white people, most of whom probably do not realize that they are doing anything wrong, make racist comments or innuendos was succinctly summarized by a white editor: "I find myself often in the position of either trying to correct people and being accused of hypersensitivity or biting my tongue and feeling like a coward." This is a Hobson's choice only if one wants to be free of risks. The question to be answered is this: "Would you prefer to suffer the agony that often comes with being accused of hypersensitivity or the agony of allowing the labeling to go unchallenged at the expense of your conscience?" On the one hand, if people speak out, they may be publicly criticized and privately condemned. On the other hand, if they remain silent, they may find the onus of their complicity emotionally devastating. Most whites opt for private devastation. Individuals who "do nothing" are actually doing something: they are allowing the negative behavior to go unchallenged, thereby giving the perpetrator a false sense of support from the silent "objectors." Action is required. Racist jokes and remarks can be countered with something such as "What you said is offensive to me, and it demeans the group you are talking about. Please refrain from telling me these things." By speaking out against labeling, the offending person(s) may actually take your comment to heart: "I never thought about it in that way. Thanks for calling it to my attention. I'll try not to do it again." If not, you can lodge a formal complaint. There are local, state, and federal laws that prohibit individuals from telling jokes and making statements that demean ethnic groups, particularly in the workplace. All employees are responsible for keeping hate out of the workplace (Solomon 1992).

Part III

Conclusion

Chapter 7

Black and
White Together

No democratic nation can reach its full potential without
providing equal opportunities to all its citizens. Furthermore, social order is maintained and violence is prevented
or curtailed by the equitable functioning of the basic institutions of society—education, employment, housing, law
enforcement, and health care in particular. Evidence of
racial discrimination within any of these institutions is a
symptom of a failed democracy.

The Past Is Prologue

Although many aspects of American society might correctly be described by the phrase "man's inhumanity to
man," none seems more worthy of this designation than
race relations in general and black-white relations in particular. Whites who deny this tend to do so from the height
of their great socioeconomic distance above black Americans. Whites who demur almost always point with pride
to a few blacks they know or know about, usually individuals who have succeeded in the performing arts or athletic endeavors. These exceptional blacks belie a nation
that at times seems indifferent to the plight of its black
citizens, a nation that does not, many African Americans
believe, really care about people of color, but only pre-
tends to.

News stories of corporate incidents of racial discrimination, burnt churches and other random and nonrandom hate crimes, and politicians passing laws to roll back civil rights provisions add fuel to a smoldering race relations fire. Once again, the United States is being torn into black and white fragments. Mainly focusing on affirmative action programs, demagogues are successfully raising the specter of a failed free enterprise system. The effect of these tirades on white Americans was evident in a 1997 Gallup poll. When asked if affirmative action programs should be increased, kept the same, or decreased, 53 percent of blacks (compared with only 22 percent of whites) thought they should be increased; 37 percent of whites and only 12 percent of blacks said they should be decreased. Almost one-third (29 percent) of both groups thought the programs should be kept the same.

In 1997 Congressman J. C. Watts said in an interview with Brent Staples, a writer for the *New York Times,* "We shouldn't fight [racial] discrimination with [reverse discrimination], but this country has not reached a level playing field. You can't get rid of affirmative action until you have something to replace it." This statement would have hardly been newsworthy if a liberal black Democrat had said it. But coming from the lone black Republican in Congress—and a conservative—it was evident that Democrats and Republicans, liberals and conservatives are deeply split on the issue of affirmative action. The "poster persons" of antiaffirmative action programs are occupationally successful blacks who claim to have made their way to the top without the benefit of special privileges. Almost always, their rags to riches tales are embellished with half-truths or outright fabrications.

Every year that the war against racism drags on, the pained victims cry out for at least a truce, but none seems forthcoming. During the period of October 1, 1995, to October 1, 1996, for example, one-third of the 78,000 workplace bias complaints filed with the U.S. Equal Employment Opportunity Commission were based on race, largely allegations filed by black Americans. This was not a statistical aberration. Two nationwide polls taken in 1996 by the Gallup Organization for *USA Today* concluded that 72 percent of the respondents believed racial discrimination against blacks in the United States was serious, and 52 percent of the respondents rated the nation's race relations as being bad. The appalling conditions within black communities that give rise to such malaise cannot be dismissed by fair-minded persons as irrelevant or insignificant: poverty continues to be a pernicious condition of a disproportionate number of black Americans, especially women and children; high school dropout rates, which are 17 percent nationally, are 30 to 40 percent in some inner-city schools; blacks are among the last persons hired and the first fired or laid off; more black males than white males under the age of sixteen have guns than computers.

The consequences of the inability of a disproportionate number of blacks to avoid failure is, as was noted earlier, also seen in criminal justice statistics.

It costs more to incarcerate adult offenders and to provide custodial care for juvenile offenders than to send them to a top-quality college—approximately $25,000 per year for each adult offender and $65,000 per year for each juvenile offender. Incarceration is anything but an effective way of rehabilitating or treating offenders. In fact, incarceration of juvenile offenders is an on-the-job training program for "wannabe" criminals. Joe Martinez, a former inmate at Indiana State Prison, wrote the following insightful parable about rehabilitation and treatment:

> The convict strolled into the prison administration building to get assistance and counseling for his personal problems. Just inside the main door were several other doors proclaiming: *Parole, Counselor, Chaplain, Doctor, Teacher, Correction,* and *Therapist.*
> The convict chose the door marked *Correction,*

inside of which were two other doors: *Custody* and *Treatment*. He chose *Treatment*, and was confronted with two more doors, *Juvenile* and *Adult*. He chose the proper door and was again faced with two doors: *Previous Offender* and *First Offender*. Once more he walked through the correct door, and again found two doors: *Democrat* and *Republican*. He was a Democrat, and so he hurried through that door and ran smack into two more doors: *Black* and *White*. He was black; and so he walked through that door—and fell nine stories to the street.

This is the experience most black Americans have over and over again—hopefully opening doors that seem to promise entry into mainstream American society only to find themselves faced with more and more doors until, ultimately, they fall into the pit racism digs for them. And it is racism—as much as we prefer not to talk about it—and one of the consequences is a rise in both black militancy and white hate groups. Citing black Americans' numerous failures and the paucity of positive role models or mentors, black militants loudly plead their case for racial separation. For the most part, this plea falls on deaf ears. Few black Americans believe that separation from mainstream white Americans will lead to much more than additional inequities. It is questionable, however, how long blacks as a whole will remain nonviolent under current conditions. Inflaming the situation, of course, are formally organized white American hate groups. The most successful hatemongers are masters of public posturing. That is, in the cutthroat competition for followers, they appeal to an audience's primal instinct to reject people who are culturally different from themselves. Beyond the public posturing of racial bigots lie age-old demons: intolerance, ignorance, and, most of all, deceit. It will take more than wishful thinking to put race relations right side up.

Hate groups are not the only racists to be feared, however. As I discussed in the previous chapter, a more subtle, covert racism has emerged, one that is not exposed by current survey data that document a significant lessening of whites publicly expressing negative beliefs about blacks. "It's crude to call [African Americans] 'niggers' or 'jungle bunnies' or 'coons,'" a white police officer told a white recruit. "But if they get out of line, you should beat the black off them." Behind the automatic smiles and willing handshakes are the new racists: persons who are suave and deceptively dangerous to gullible blacks. And they are fairly evenhanded in their bigotry. They dislike "nigger-loving whites," too. We should not delude ourselves into believing that along with declining overt negative attitudes of whites toward blacks in opinion polls has come a proportionate decline in covert racist beliefs. Good words spoken to pollsters do not equate with an end to racism. Good behaviors must also occur.

Justice for All

Whatever opportunities have accrued to black Americans, to date relatively few individuals, mainly upwardly mobile males, have benefited, and tokenism has never been the best remedy for mass inequalities. Compared with affluent blacks, poverty-stricken black Americans need more than a fair measure of justice, and certainly more than tokenism. America can and must do better. A just society will find socially redemptive ways to salvage its wasted citizens. And it will use humane methods.

Specifically, programs for providing quality education and adequate employment for blacks should include pre-school and early education activities aimed at compensating for early experiential deficits, primarily in language and cognitive development; remedial programs in basic job skills, including individual and small-group tutoring conducted by well-trained professionals, paraprofessionals, and peers; enrichment programs to overcome negative cultural differences, enhance motivation, and otherwise widen the horizons of blacks from low-income families; preservice and in-service training of school and corporate personnel to familiarize them with the lifestyles of black Americans; and special guidance programs to extend counseling services to children and adults. When this is done, more blacks will achieve the American dream.

Those who are about the business of righting wrongs bear the burden of making operative the Pledge of Allegiance—one nation with liberty and justice for *all*. Is this a hackneyed approach? Perhaps it is, but so, too, is racial discrimination.

Coalitions against Racism

The concerned persons—teachers, supervisors, and citizens—described throughout this book share the characteristic of *personal involvement* that emanates from their feelings of outrage at the behaviors of hateful people, from their need to communicate grievances, and from their need to get rid of injustices. The significant question for whites who wish to become actively involved in improving black-white relations is not "What would, could, or should you do if you had more time, wealth, or resources?" Instead, it is "What are you willing to do with the time, wealth, or resources you have now?"

In the absence of broad-scale group initiatives, change can only occur through individual or group actions, though ultimately, it will be in coalitions, not as a result of isolated individual actions, that progress is likely to be made toward eliminating racism. Coalitions embody a very old legal safeguard which has come down to us through English common law: "standing." It is impossible for all citizens to be heard when community decisions are being made or challenged, but a group of dedicated persons who possess great understanding of the issues in question can use "standing" to speak on behalf of all persons similarly aggrieved. The foundation of a successful black-white coalition is the will of its members to unrelentingly seek racial equality. And they must have the backbone to endure ridicule from people who believe that such organizational efforts are futile.

A coalition against racism should not be limited to clichés about brotherhood or sisterhood; these appeals have been falling on deaf ears for years. If America is to survive, all citizens must reconcile themselves to living together peacefully, because the alternative is disastrous. And they must live together not with platitudes, but with helpful action.

In order for whites and blacks to successfully conspire to bring about change, honest and open dialogue is needed, as are creative black-white coalitions. The most successful civil rights coalitions have been neighborhood or community groups convened by concerned citizens to address a current problem that can be resolved in a relatively short time frame. The characteristics of successful black-white coalitions are two-way communication, cooperation, and mutual respect. These are rare qualities in any alliance, let alone those that are interracial. In the best organizations communication among members is open and is unaffected by race or power; decisions are based on consensus rather than on coercion or compromise; and influence is based on technical competence and knowledge rather than on hierarchy.

All interracial coalitions experience periods of turmoil. If one racial group always gives in to the other, conflict will be suppressed but present. The longer the conflict remains hidden, the greater the tension. Because conflict is inevitable, conflict resolution is a never-ending process. Some individuals quit at the first sign of altercation; they are fair-weather members. Others deny there is conflict; they are delusional. The pretense that there is complete harmony can destroy the sense of sincerity found in effective black-white coalitions. François La Rochefoucauld (1936) remarked in *Maxims* that "sincerity is a revelation of the heart. One finds it in very few people; what one usually finds is but a clever pretense made to gain the confidence of others" (44).

Trust is at the heart of the matter. Coalition members who trust each other freely admit their feelings, whatever they may be, because they have a sense of togetherness. Also, they are flexible in making proposals and accepting counterproposals to resolve conflict. The following incident illustrates one of the challenges a black-white coalition faces. It also illustrates the level of patience and self-control required to get past sudden angry flare-ups.

One Hundred Families is an ad hoc association of black and white families who live in an upper-middle-income neighborhood. It is dedicated to stabilizing the neighborhood by stemming an exodus of white home owners. Organized in 1990, the association has been able to maintain a ratio of approximately 70 white and 30 black home owners. One day Rick, a black member of the association, angrily asked Tim, a white member, why he did not use his influence to get the school board to remove from next month's agenda a plan to rezone the neighborhood elementary school out of its predominantly white district into a predominantly black district, which feeds its elementary schools into predominantly black middle schools.

"I never agreed to do that," Tim replied. "We never decided as an organization that I should! Besides, we [the association] have to decide whether or not it's best for the community to have our children in that zone."

"Then I guess I'm lying, huh?" Rick snarled.

Tim could feel his jaw tightening. He sucked hard to get his breath and maintain composure.

"I'm lying, huh?" Rick repeated.

"You're...."

"I'm what?" Rick cut him off. "Be careful what you say, Tim. Don't let your mouth get your butt in trouble."

Tim had never seen this side of Rick. He was obviously very angry and his words and body posture were threatening. Tim's first impulse was to respond in kind—let Rick know that he couldn't push this white guy around. Instead, he lowered his voice, looked Rick in the eyes, and said, "This isn't a case of who's lying and who's telling the truth. This is a case of both of us thinking the other person said something he didn't. Why don't we put the issue [of rezoning] to the other members?" The tone of Tim's voice and his look of sincerity caused Rick to rescind the charge that Tim had double-crossed him. "Okay, let's do it at the next meeting."

Often, in the heat of adversarial exchanges, men, especially, try to win arguments through intimidation rather than diplomacy. The situation is even more volatile when the argument is between a black man and a white man. Both may feel the need to prove their manhood. Here, destructive conflict was avoided when Tim decided not to respond to Rick's tirade with his own anger. Pettiness and one-upmanship would have been counterproductive in this situation and could have resulted in Tim and Rick embarrassing each other.

Unbridled anger can breach coalitions. Strong black-white coalitions are similar to strong marriages. Unless the members are constantly dealing with their anger, relationships will atrophy. The joy of achieving conflict resolution in race relations is often purchased at a high price, but it is a price that enriches, rather than impoverishes, the participants.

Emotionally interdependent blacks and whites readily admit their need for support from each other. When they bond together in this manner, they give and receive support, they interlock their lives, and they become the equivalent of brothers and sisters. This type of relationship is the sturdiest foundation on which to build a campaign against racism. Coalition members get a lot done, but they often ruffle feathers in the process. Some of them become the rebels Mari E. Evans wrote about:

When I
die
I'm sure
I will have a
Big Funeral...
Curiosity
seekers...
coming to see
if I
am really
Dead...
or just
trying to make
Trouble....

—"The Rebel"
Mari E. Evans

A question frequently asked is: "What can I do in my community to improve black-white relations?" The answer must necessarily be decided by each person. In some cases a coalition may be the optimal choice; in others, individual action may be called for. The following checklist will be helpful.

1. Which places in your community are racially segregated?
2. What ways have you resisted efforts to integrate blacks into your neighborhood, schools, place of religious worship, workplace, or social organizations?
3. What institutional practices, such as redlining, real estate covenants, public school district boundaries, and club membership criteria, contribute to racial segregation in your community?
4. In which ways do the schools in your community perpetuate misinformation and inadequate knowledge of African Americans?
5. What have you done to challenge racially oppressive conditions in your community?
   a. Have your efforts cost you emotionally, socially, or economically?

b. What additional information or skills do you need to be optimally effective in combating racism?

The complex, mercurial conditions that characterize black-white relations in the United States often leave the participants unsure of what to do next. The title of a Thomas A. Dorsey song, "Standing Here Wonderin' Which Way to Go," epitomizes their hesitancy. One thing is evident, however: one cannot do nothing. Even inaction has consequences. And every action in an interpersonal black-white encounter is a relevant movement in the societal game of race relations. The endgame is a nation free of racial intolerance.

There's Room at the Table

The number of civil rights activists is small and becoming even smaller. Nonetheless, their tenacity and intransigent commitment to racial justice give the illusion of a considerably larger group. They are iconoclasts who seem to thrive on adversity, matching wits with bigots at the outer edge of civility. Only an individual who has been one knows how socially precarious life can be for civil rights activists. Relatedly, only people who have been the beneficiaries of the activists' deeds can fully appreciate their positive contributions to race relations. Whatever their strengths or weaknesses, civil rights activists are often the fulcrum of social change. Accused by some blacks of doing too little to help blacks and by many whites of doing too much to hurt whites, activists have never had an easy time of it.

Many of the new activists feel more comfortable (and are actually more useful) working with computers and spreadsheets than participating in public protest activities such as picket lines. This is okay. There is a need for the broadest array of skills in order to get more blacks into workstations, college and vocational classrooms, neighborhoods, and social clubs. People who generate, analyze, and publish data are needed to provide accurate reports that give credence to those who protest the paucity of blacks in certain community roles. "There's a place for lots of people at the civil rights table," a black minister once told a white geologist.

Most white civil rights activists seem to be comfortable as community change agents when they are involved in (1) securing appointments for blacks in political and civic associations, (2) desegregating schools, and (3) getting blacks jobs in places where they are noticeably absent or underrepresented. Less often, however, do white activists wholeheartedly advocate desegregation of their neighborhoods and places of worship, which is the basis for an old saying within the black community: "Most white Americans don't care how high [successful] we [black Americans] get [in jobs and education] as long as we don't get too close [to them in housing and religious services]." In fact, the most racially segregated places in America are houses, churches, synagogues, and mosques. "We don't have to guess who's not invited to dinner or prayer meetings in a white community. It's us," a black nurse told a group of white nurses in a workshop focusing on race relations.

But even when blacks are invited to dinner by "concerned" whites, the result is often merely polite, intellectual dinner chatter that sounds like so much blather, not a substantive racial encounter.

> I know I am
> The Negro Problem
> Being wined and dined
> Answering the usual questions
> That come to white mind
> Which seeks demurely
> To probe in polite way
> The why and wherewithal
> Of darkness U.S.A.—
> Wondering how things got this way
> In current democratic night,
> Murmuring gently
> Over *fraises du bois*,
> "I'm so ashamed of being white."

The lobster is delicious
The wine divine,
And center of attention
At the damask table, mine.
To be a Problem on
Park Avenue at eight
Is not so bad
Solutions to the Problem,
Of course, wait.
—"Dinner Guest: Me"
Langston Hughes

With few exceptions, blacks who have joined the ranks of the economically successful have had to make their way up the hierarchal ladder from the "wrong side of the tracks." Dinners and other social activities with whites were gratifying, but to get to the top in the workplace, they received support, not food or verbiage from whites.

Even black naysayers admit that within the arenas of employment and education anyway, black and white coalitions have been moderately successful, and no one can dispute the importance of whites, especially Catholic, Jewish, and Protestant leaders, in civil rights activities. In order for significantly more change to occur, however, blacks must want it, white liberals must support it, and whites in power must agree to it. The argument made by black civil rights leaders in the 1960s and 1970s is still valid: it is unrealistic for America to expect poor black people to pull themselves up by their bootstraps when few of them have boots. Black Americans need the assistance of white Americans. And that assistance requires more volunteers. No black American has ever achieved a breakthrough in a white community—in a school or a job or anything else— without the assistance of at least one white person. Large numbers of white change agents are not required, but those who are involved must have the power to influence or actually make the change happen.

Effective whites know that *it is behaviors, not attitudes, that constitute the major race relations problems confront-*

ing black Americans. There are many laws against discriminatory behaviors, but there are none against prejudicial attitudes.

There is a place at the table for all persons, including loyalist whites hiding in organizations—people afraid of losing their Establishment jobs and social status but wanting to save their souls. By concealing their empathy for blacks, they too can contribute by giving the appearance of being completely objective when recommending qualified blacks for jobs and promotions or by acting as anonymous whistle-blowers, providing appropriate officials with information about civil rights violations. There is also a place for blacks who are passing for white, people hiding their true identity. Indeed, there is a place at the table for anyone whose sense of right-mindedness compels him or her to do whatever is possible to create a just society. When these civil rights undercover agents are mobilized, the final phase of a battle begun hundreds of years ago will commence: eradication of America's black-white racial divide.

The major task that remains for concerned whites and blacks alike is to help the black underclass escape environmental squalor and rid themselves of the sense of hopelessness that characterizes their lives. In the process of doing this, white Americans must not let their racial fears, rivalry with blacks, and conflicting community loyalties cause them to lose sight of the task. Equality of opportunity for all is a truly humanitarian goal, the kind that needs no apology.

As a black university professor told an all-white crowd:

> In order for there to be a revitalized civil rights movement, more white women, once vocal members in civil rights coalitions, must return and bring their daughters with them. More white men, especially those in other human rights organizations, must reclaim their place at the civil rights table and bring their sons. Middle-class black men and women who

live in predominantly white neighborhoods and communities must take time out from their exclusive club privileges and white dinner-guest notoriety long enough to be true champions for their underclass brothers and sisters. Yes, the clarion call must be heeded by those who are tired of being frontline warriors, those who are afraid to be, and those who dare not to be.

Unsung Heroes

There is little doubt that the nation is at a crossroads in its race relations. Where we go from here is up to all of us— blacks and whites together. We can try segregation again, continuance of the status quo, silence in the face of prejudice and discriminatory practices, or activism. The choice is ours.

Segregation of blacks is not a redeeming choice for America. It did not work during earlier times, and it will not work now. There have never been separate but equal white and black communities in the United States. And the pretense of such a condition would once again be a particularly pernicious injustice to all citizens. Racial segregation diminishes both the perpetrators and the victims. Preserving the status quo in education, employment, and housing, which so often is little more than codified racial discrimination, is not justice for blacks either.

Inaction by people who witness oppressive acts is equally unacceptable. Even though they may be shocked and frustrated by the problems, standing in wide-eyed horror is not an adequate posture to assume. While they may be legally absolved of any wrongdoing, these silent people must come to terms with what others believe to be their moral culpability. Of course, silence may be prudent. Usually, there is a high price to be paid by those who would challenge racism in community institutions. Friends, jobs, promotions, and prestige may be lost. Furthermore, few victories come easy and most of the victors are unsung heroes.

Individuals who choose to speak out must also take care that in their actions to redress racial injustices, they do not emulate the oppressors whom they deplore. That might makes right, that blood washes out injustices, these too are false strategies for achieving justice. "It does not matter much to a slave what the color of his master is," a wise black janitor once said.

Obviously, concerned individuals must also be realists when trying to alter the course of black-white relations:

> Shallow activism...must be changed into a considerably deeper and more sophisticated sense of involvement. This calls for listening to people outside one's own myopic clique as well as sober examination of righteousness in one's motives and actions. A realist throws away rose-colored glasses, straightens his shoulders and looks freely about him in all directions. He wants to see whatever there is to see, in relation to other people and things as well as to himself. A realist alone comprehends hope. Optimism is as antithetical to authentic hope as pessimism. Hope is rooted in realism (Boyd 1971, 128).

Improved race relations requires the interaction of realists but not those who are detached and passionless onlookers. The civil rights movement began when impassioned black and white citizens challenged racists. It will continue with similar realistic but passionate behavior. Sometimes, as Reverend Bill tells this story, the Holy Spirit moves people to do passionate things they might not otherwise dare contemplate.

> It started out like any other Sunday morning worship service. I got to the church early so that I could greet members of the congregation as they filed in—like willing soldiers of the Lord. As usual, Sister Beard, the only black member of our tiny Baptist church, was one of the first to arrive.

> Word has it that eighty-year-old Sister Beard joined our church ten years before I became pastor. She was tired of trying to get a ride to a black church in a nearby city. And it was almost impossible for her to

get transportation to out-of-town Wednesday night services. So she joined our church, even though, as she constantly reminded us, there wasn't much rhythm in the lot of us. And my sermons, she quietly advised me, could use "a little fire." "Heat us up," she would tell me. I looked forward to seeing Sister Beard, with her smiling eyes and once-proud body. There was a certain dignity about her.

"Are you going to heat us up this morning, Reverend Bill?" she asked as she shook my hand and moved down to the second row, right-side pew, third seat from the inner aisle.

Shortly thereafter, Ralph and his wife and two children came in. "Morning, Reverend," he gripped my hand and squeezed as though it was a contest of strength.

I struggled to free my hand from his viselike grip. "I haven't seen much of you this year, Ralph," I said, looking at his frowning face.

"Church ain't been the same since we turned liberal," he responded, pointing to Sister Beard.

I didn't answer Ralph, but I'm sure he noticed my disgust. The walk down the aisle to my seat behind the pulpit seemed to take longer that day. When the time came for me to deliver the sermon, I put aside the cards on which I had written the outline of my message.

The sermon I delivered came from me, but the outline was written by God. I started with Luke 10:22, talked about loving people who are racially different, and I ended with Romans 13:8 and this message to Sister Beard: "I love you and I am glad you are a member of this church."

Tears streamed down both our cheeks. Someone shouted "Amen" and others followed. The choir sang its concluding song, and they seemed to have more soul and rhythm that morning.

On the way out of the church, Sister Beard grabbed my hands and smiled, "You sure heated us up today, Reverend."

Ralph's wife, Lillian, came by at that moment. She looked at me and said "Amen." And while Ralph was trying to corral one of their children, she reached over and hugged Sister Beard.

Two years later, Ralph transferred his membership to another church—an all-white one. Three years later, Lillian filed for divorce and returned to our church with her two children.

Sometimes the price for being an unsung hero can be painfully high, requiring personal sacrifice. A black college professor recalled such a sacrifice.

The real estate agencies had an unwritten (and illegal) covenant not to sell property to blacks. Consequently, when I decided to accept a teaching position at the university, I had no idea why my wife and I could not easily find a house, although the real estate listings had several that were within our budget and met our family's needs. After two unsuccessful attempts to purchase a house, I notified the president of the university that I regretfully would not be able to honor my contract because I was unable to secure a house. In fact, the realtors who told me that my first and second choices were sold also informed me that all other choices were sold, which they were not. By then the word had spread throughout the real estate offices: do not sell *him* [me] a house.

The president of the university informed the chair of the Sociology Department and the dean of the College of Education of my predicament. He also asked them to help me find a house. After a frantic scouring of the community, the chair of the Sociology Department found a cooperative realtor who in turn found a willing seller, a university staff member who was moving to another location. I bought a house.

My family and I were subjected to considerable hostility. The university staff member whose house I purchased was accosted for selling his house to a "nigger" and "destroying property values" in the neighborhood. The realtor was even more severely sanctioned. Her customers withdrew their contracts and few new customers were added. In less than three years, she was forced out of business. When I asked her why she sacrificed her business to sell me a house, she said something that gave me a new perspective on white liberals: "Losing my real estate office was a small price to pay. If I had not sold you that house, I would have lost much more: my self-respect."

We Need Another Dream

For more than three decades, countless Americans have pursued the dream eloquently enunciated by Martin Luther King Jr.—that racial segregation and discrimination will be abolished. At the historic 1963 March on Washington, his words became the philosophical underpinning for black-white coalitions. Ironically, portions of Dr. King's "I Have a Dream" speech have been taken out of context and used by individuals (whom he probably would have called antagonists) to champion antiaffirmative action legislation. Specifically, they cite Dr. King's reference to judging people by the quality of their character instead of the color of their skin to justify abolishing so-called "reverse discrimination" programs. What especially riles civil rights activists about this initiative is the assertion that the human rights "playing field" is now level and ethnic minorities no longer need to be treated as a protected class in government-monitored programs. Contrary to popular notion, blacks are not yet "free at last."

Scores of pending civil rights lawsuits throughout the United States suggest that there is still a need for government oversight in education and employment. Americans have yet to enact a social justice contract that will humanely bind blacks and whites together as human beings of equal worth. Even more disheartening is the fact that for many lower-income and all underclass black Americans, life is little or no better than before. They continue to be in harm's way from sunup until sundown. Life for them is a frightening and emotionally painful nightmare from which they cannot wake up. Feelings of anguish, abandonment, and despair are reasonable responses to negative physical or social conditions.

But underclass blacks should not be encouraged to dwell in the quietism of despair. These individuals need cheerleaders, not pallbearers. That is, they need to be told that there is in all of us a wide range of abilities and potentialities which are unused but still viable, and which cannot be inferred from one's previous behaviors or current community circumstances. Also, they need help to navigate bureaucratic rules and regulations—not just from whites but from middle-class blacks as well.

Both older and younger generations of black Americans agree that there is currently a need for a new national dream focusing on the twenty-first century. Much has changed for the better since Dr. King's historic speech in 1963. Numerous civil rights laws have been enacted, and it is unlikely that most of them will be repealed, but most agree that "we still ain't what we wanta be," in the words of an old Negro saying:

We ain't what we wanta be,
We ain't what we aughta be,
And we ain't what we gonna be,
But, thank God,
We ain't what we was.

In order to get to the "what we gonna be" stage, a new dream, or vision, is needed to supplement and complement Dr. King's dream. Things have changed. Consider, for example, the fact that the number of biracial marriages and children are increasing at a rapid rate each year. In 1997 about one in thirty-nine marriages in the United States was interracial—three and a half times as many as in 1972. During that twenty-five-year period, approximately one million interracial American children were born in wedlock, and probably another million were born out of wedlock.

White Americans' attitudes on black-white marriages have shifted dramatically as well. A 1997 Gallup poll found that for the first time since it asked the question in 1958, the majority (61 percent) of white respondents approved of marriage between blacks and whites. (In 1958 only 4 percent approved; in 1994 the approval rate had increased to 45 percent.) The new dream needs to encompass more than just black-white or other majority-minority issues. A sizable number of Americans are "shadow people," individuals whose true identities are subsumed under a category that forces them to choose an "official" racial or ethnic designation which ignores some or all members of their own family, or the nondescriptive and socially demeaning category, "other." An inquisitive college freshman made the following statement during a race relations rally:

> There are lots of us in this country who are being forced to deny a parent and sometimes half our relatives. We're not just African Americans or Caucasians; we're part of each. My mother is part African American and part German American. My father is part Mexican and part French American. I check the box "Other" on the university forms because I can only select one category. But by checking that category, I am officially nothing.... My family members are blacks and whites. Is America going to go back to the "one drop Negro blood" classification? What am I?...

A sarcastic black female student in the audience shouted out, "You're confused, sister." Amid the laughter that followed, another black student spoke out more insightfully, "You're the next generation of Americans—you're all of your people." With sudden compassion, the mood of the audience changed from levity and ridicule to consternation. There was nothing in their curriculums or previous academic dialogues to adequately prepare the students to think beyond discrete racial or ethnic designations. Suddenly, although this had been fermenting for years, the students were being asked to go beyond the civil rights issues that are neatly cast as black or white. They were not sure how to handle this situation, so a speaker on the stage said, "That [discussion] is not why we are here. We are here to get more rights for black people." When they drifted back into the narrowly circumscribed (and more comfortable) issues—how to get more black students, faculty, staff, and courses—a defining problem came and went without adequate attention.

Too often, Americans write race relations dramas and paint race relations murals depicting whites and blacks as the lead actors and primary subjects, with only occasional representatives of other groups as peripheral participants. This is a distortion of reality. Too much emphasis is placed on *race* relations and not enough on *human* relations. If we accept the premise that in a democratic nation the only race of any significance is the human race, then we need leaders who can move our social justice agenda beyond race. "Why," a black female asked a white friend, "are you able to be comfortable with me when so many of my own people are turned off by my dark [skin] color and [physical] features?" Her friend thought about the question for a long time before answering: "Beneath your color and physical features is the essence of you—a warm, caring person. I looked beyond your skin to find you." America must look beyond race and ethnicity to find its identity.

Some civil rights activists do not believe that racial integration is a viable goal. The integration or desegregation polarities are specious. Both should be choices—including positions in between. "We couldn't get into the melting pot with the other people and melt into 'Americans' like white ethnics did many years ago," black civil rights leaders continually remind the nation. Lately, another view is being offered to counter the historical rejection. In Chicago, that view was offered by a white dentist: "We've got a new pot and new cooks. Those who want to be gumbo [integrated] can do so. Those who want to remain an entree [distinct ethnic groups] can do so. There is a need for variety at the new dinner table of democracy." Perhaps neither multiculturalism nor integration is the best answer to the race division. Cultural pluralism may be a better option. That is, we can both celebrate our cultural differences and build a nation based on our commonalities—common core cultural values, beliefs, and behaviors that support justice for all.

As the nation moves further into the postmodern era, we will indeed need new and courageous leaders—and new dreams. It would be foolish to expect the new leaders to be a homogeneous group. They will come from the ranks of liberals, moderates, and conservatives; Democrats, Republicans, Libertarians, members of the Reform Party, and other political parties; the religious and the nonreligious; rich, middle income, and poor—a potpourri of Americans. Foremost among the new dreams must be visions of a society where all people can have safe housing, get a top-quality education, do meaningful work for adequate wages, and die a timely death unhurried by any "ism." Individuals who facilitate the achievement of that dream will feel a profound sense of accomplishment. And, surely, if they should die before they wake, the Lord their souls will take.

Afterword

The Middle Passage:
Autobiographical
Continuation

My rapprochement with white people has had both en-
lightening and unexpected twists and turns.

All of my teachers, elementary school through high
school, were white. A handful of caring, talented teachers
helped me to be the first person in my family to graduate
from high school. Those teachers did a fantastic job in-
stilling in me the desire to get good grades. But they failed
to teach me or my classmates to be racially tolerant. Sadly,
blacks and whites merely occupied the same physical space
during school hours. There were even separate lunch
groups and playground cliques. The only significant interactions I had with my white classmates were in required
formal school activities. Blacks and whites did very little
together socially. In fact, I never had a close white friend.
Upon reflection, it is clear to me that I disliked most of the
white people, students and school personnel, who were in
my high school. During those days, I described my behavior as being "socially selective"; today I would call it bigotry. There was very little in my public school experiences
that prepared me for interracial activities in the college of
my choice: Michigan State Agricultural and Mechanical
College (several years later the name was changed to Michi-

gan State University). My journey to Michigan State was the beginning of a memorable odyssey.

I knew that Michigan State had approximately 12,000 students, but I was surprised upon my arrival on campus to find out that fewer than fifty of them were blacks. Throughout the first year, most of my time was spent overcoming culture shock, establishing close ties with the other black students, being a pledge in a black fraternity, and trying to maintain a *B* grade point average in order to keep my student-athlete scholarship. All of my social time was spent with blacks. Early in the second year, however, I was shaken out of my comfort zone. It started out quietly enough. I was the first person to check into my dormitory room and I used the early arrival as an opportunity to select the best bed. While I was putting some of my clothes in a dresser drawer, the room door opened and my new roommate entered. I was speechless. Stoically standing in front of me was a tall, country-looking white student. I gathered my composure, glared at him, and snarled, "Damn if I'm gonna stay in this room with you."

Before I could start another sentence, he snapped at me, "You better believe you ain't goin' to be in this room with me, boy."

We were almost nose to nose and ready to use our fists to settle whose room it was. A dormitory counselor overheard the shouting and came to check on us. "What's going on in here?" he asked as he gently pushed us away from each other. My assigned roommate and I said that neither of us wanted to be with the other. The counselor calmly advised us that one of Michigan State's housing regulations forbids room changes merely because the roommates don't like each other. He further explained that the policy prevents roommates from "disappearing." The regulation was passed a couple of years earlier after two black students complained about white students who checked into their room, discovered that their roommates were black, checked out, and were reassigned white roommates.

"The Lord works in mysterious ways," Papa (my mother's father) often told me when I was a small child. Whether or not the Lord was responsible for this situation is debatable. But one thing was evident: a black bigot and a white bigot were irrevocably assigned to the same room. Unable to convince the housing director to reassign us, George, my roommate, and I decided to make the best of a bad situation by being civil to each other. Within a short period of time our conversations changed from casual, polite banter to intense, often heated, discussions of racial issues. I don't remember exactly when the other white students joined in our "bull sessions," but on any given weekday night, there would be six or seven white guys and me crammed into the tiny room exploring and exploding racial myths and stereotypes. We wrestled with our own ignorance and bigotry. Through that process, the enemies got to know each other as human beings of equal worth. Indeed, I learned more about white people during those interactions than I did from all the undergraduate courses I took.

One night in particular stands out in my mind. It was around midnight. George and I had just finished studying for midterm exams. He looked at me and sheepishly whispered, "I don't know how to ask you, but something has been bothering me for a long time.... Can I see your tail?" He had been told by one of his uncles that blacks were the missing link between great apes and humans and therefore we had an imperceptible tail. I frowned, pulled down my pajama bottom, turned my buttocks to him, and said, "There it is. Do you want to kiss it?" We both laughed as he looked for a tail. His apology to me was not nearly as important as our willingness to be honest with each other.

Midway through my junior year, I dropped out of ROTC and was classified 1-A by my local draft board. On a tip from a friend who served on the board, I decided to "beat" the draft by volunteering to serve in the Air Force, where I repaired radios at a remote site in French Morocco, North

Africa. After I got out of the Air Force, Barbara, my wife, and I moved to Detroit, Michigan. We had two children and not much of an income. I did many things to make ends meet, including being a shipping clerk in a shoe distributor warehouse, a laborer in a bakery, and a page in the main branch of the Detroit Public Library. Those jobs and my G.I. benefit money made it possible for me to pursue a bachelor's degree at Wayne University (later renamed Wayne State University). I worked full-time and attended college full-time. Although Detroit had a large, growing black population, there were relatively few (two or three) black students in the classes I attended.

One of the courses I enrolled in was entitled Introduction to Drama. The teacher was a portly, scholarly-looking middle-aged man, who promptly informed us, "I am a student of Stanislavsky, who is a master teacher of method acting." He was like no other teacher I had experienced. At the blink of an eye, he could summon scores of people from inside his rotund body. One minute his voice was soft and soothing, the next it was loud and intimidating—he could make it rise and fall with convincing consistency. My classmates called him "a one-man play for the price of tuition." Before he allowed us to read plays, we had to train our minds to become "things." We "became" rocks, chairs, cats, birds—things!

Midway through the semester, after a "rock" exercise, he told us to become trees. He smiled as we stood erect around the room with our arms extended like branches: "Try to feel like a tree. It's raining. What do you feel?" he asked us. I could feel the water soaking slowly up through my roots into my branches. I felt good, I was being nourished.

"Now, class," he said loudly, "some birds are coming...they are circling overhead." Oh, no, I thought. Don't let them. I could feel the tension and fear within. My worst fear came true with these words from the teacher: "A bird has landed on one of your branches and it is pecking it. Now, what do you feel?" I hurt! I hurt bad. The bird was destroying a part of me. Perhaps sensing our pain, he said: "That's enough of this exercise, class. You were marvelous trees and before that you were magnificent rocks. Last week some of you were sensitive cats. I have but one question: why do you have so much difficulty being human beings?" As if struck by a bolt of insight, I then understood the act of empathy. I could, if I sincerely tried, understand most people of other ethnic, income, gender, and age groups, to mention a few. It was not the ability that I lacked but the will.

After graduating with a bachelor's degree in sociology in 1957, I got a job as a social caseworker. With Barbara's encouragement, I decided to apply for admission to the master's degree program in sociology at Wayne State. The most agonizing experience I had that year was getting my Graduate Record Examination scores. They almost completely shattered my confidence. Fortunately, Dr. Leonard Moss, chairman of the Anthropology and Sociology Department, decided to disregard the low test scores and admit me on probation. "I want you to prove to me and yourself that you are not those scores," he said, pointing to the GRE printout. He and three other white professors became my mentors. One of them, Dr. Frank Hartung, a renowned criminologist, got me involved in research projects and also asked me to critique his book manuscript. All of my mentors required (and got) top-quality course work from me. Whenever I became anxiety-ridden about an assignment, Dr. Moss would admonish me: "I don't want to hear about what you can't do. Let's talk about what you can and will do." He neither encouraged nor tolerated my self-flagellations. Nor would he let me use white racism as a reason to do poor-quality work. To reward me for earning good grades, Dr. Moss paid for me to attend an American Sociological Association annual conference that was held in Evanston, Illinois, where he proudly introduced me to famous scholars, including Drs.

Robert Merton, Talcott Parsons, and E. Franklin Frazier. Someday, I said to myself, I will be a professor.

In 1960, one year after I received a master's degree in sociology, I became a social economist in the Detroit Housing Commission. In that job I established contact with indigenous black leaders who lived in low-income neighborhoods. In 1961, impressed with my work within black communities, the director of the Detroit Urban League appointed me community services assistant. That was the beginning of my active involvement in the Civil Rights Movement. Whitney Young Jr., executive director of the National Urban League, became a friend and mentor. He got me involved in numerous civil rights projects, including campaigns to feed poor, inner-city children and programs to train freedom riders—people who traveled to the South to assist blacks in voting and in boycotting racial discrimination. Through those activities I met Martin Luther King Jr. (Southern Christian Leadership Conference), Malcolm X (Nation of Islam), and Roy Wilkins (NAACP). Identified by key politicians as being a "black intellectual" and a "community activist," I became an informal adviser to several prominent Michigan political leaders, including Governor George Romney, Mayor Jerome Cavanaugh, and Congressman Charles Diggs.

In 1962 I was promoted to director of the Detroit Urban League's Community Service Department. From July 1963 until June 1965, I was employed in administrative positions in two projects that focused on researching and preventing juvenile delinquency.

In 1963 I enrolled in Wayne State's doctoral program in educational sociology. Although my studies progressed uneventfully during the first year, I was disgusted by the fact that there were fewer than a dozen active black doctoral students at Wayne State. The following incident gave me insight as to the reason. I turned in a term paper to a professor of educational philosophy and eagerly awaited his critique. Two weeks later he returned all of the papers except mine. The next week he stopped me as I was leaving the class and asked me to come to his office the next day. I did. He was thirty minutes late and obviously quite irritated. Rummaging through a stack of papers, he pulled out mine and threw it at me. He stared intently at me as I picked up the paper, his face cherry red. "I've been to the library several times trying to find the sources you plagiarized to write that paper, Mr. Henderson. I couldn't find them, so I won't file an academic misconduct charge against you. Take the paper and get out of my office." A big *F* was scribbled in red ink across the top of the first page. I tried to talk to him, but he would not listen.

Outside the office, a flood of emotions erupted: confusion, anger, fear. Before withdrawing from the doctoral program (a failing grade in the course would have tarnished my academic record beyond repair), I decided to seek advice from Dr. Moss. I found him in his office and told him what had happened. He asked me to let him read the paper. I stood as he read it slowly, sometimes emitting sounds such as "huh," "ah," and "shit." He pointed to the chair positioned in front of his cluttered desk and said, "I'm going to do something that's not professional, but I feel it's important to do." He picked up a telephone and called the professor who had given me the failing grade.

"This is Professor Leonard Moss," he began the conversation into the telephone. "I've found out that you gave George Henderson an *F* for a paper he wrote for you. Something about plagiarism, I believe. Well, I've read the paper and can vouch that it's George's style. I doubt very seriously that it's plagiarized. He has written papers for my classes that were much better than the one he wrote for you. Hell, I would give him a *B* for the paper he turned in to you." My heart felt like it was going to jump out of my body. I tuned out the rest of the conversation. When Dr. Moss finished the conversation, he smiled, pointed to the door, and told me to go home.

The next educational philosophy class was an eye-opener. The professor asked me to come to his office after the class ended. When I got there, he apologized for giving me an F, asked me for the paper, and crossed out the F. Then he looked at me. There were tears in his eyes. "Mr. Henderson, until I talked with Professor Moss, I had no reason to believe that you wrote the paper." He brushed away the tears and continued, "Actually, I had no reason to believe that you didn't write the paper. I am now aware that I must come to grips with my own prejudice. I didn't believe a Negro could write such a fine paper." Then he put a big red A on the paper. Driving home that night, I felt a chill go through my body. I wondered how many other white professors did not believe black students were capable of doing A work.

In 1964 Leonard Moss ("Drop the Dr.," he told me) convinced me to become an adjunct instructor and teach evening sociology courses at Wayne State. I loved teaching the courses and almost all of the students enjoyed them too—at least that is what the course evaluations indicated. The next semester I was asked to teach sociology courses at Michigan State and the University of Michigan.

After receiving my doctorate in 1965, I became an assistant director of intercultural relations in the Detroit Public Schools. One year later I became an assistant to the superintendent, Dr. Norman Drachler.

In January 1967, Leonard called me to his office and said, "It's time for you to make an honest man of yourself. You're one of the best teachers I have known—regular faculty or part-time. Why don't you stop moonlighting and become a full-time teacher?" In May 1967, I received a telephone call from the University of Oklahoma. The person at the other end of the line said, "Dr. Henderson, how are you? I am Dick Hilbert, chairman of the Sociology Department. I heard that you are considering becoming a full-time university professor. If that's true, based on the information I have about you, I would very much like you to visit O.U. for a job interview. In order to provide a decent salary, the appointment would be in both sociology and education. Are you interested?"

In my most arrogant voice I said, "Dr. Hilbert, there's something you need to know about me."

"What is it?" he asked.

"I'm a Negro."

He laughed and answered, "That's your problem. Will you come for the lecture interview?"

After the interview, I accepted the offer to join the faculty at the University of Oklahoma. The $16,400 salary was $5,000 less than my Detroit Public Schools salary. Nevertheless, I was excited about starting a full-time teaching career in a place I did not know much about before the lecture interview. The only thing I really knew about O.U. was that it had good football teams. Until shortly before the visit I did not even know where the university was located. Whatever my decision was—daring or foolish or daringly foolish, depending on whom I talked to— I became the third black professor at O.U.'s Norman campus in August 1967, and the city of Norman's first black home owner.

"Why did you do that? Why didn't you accept one of the offers you had from the more prestigious schools?" Leonard Moss asked me. I didn't answer him.

In July 1967, before we left for Norman, rioting erupted in Detroit. A skirmish occurred two blocks from where I lived. I watched the stores on the street behind me burn as black mobs pillaged them. The violence and destruction received worldwide attention. Detroit was a city under siege. Suddenly Oklahoma seemed like a good place to be. Barbara was glad that we were moving our seven children and her mother away from the shooting, killing, burning, and looting that had come to characterize the hot July mayhem.

But the fact that we moved into a house that was our third choice was an ominous beginning. The people who lived in our first- and second-choice neighborhoods didn't want blacks living there. Apparently most of them believed their property values would go down if we moved in. Some of them even believed we would throw our barbecue bones on the front lawn and that late at night we would sneak our relatives into the house to live with us. One frightened lady believed that I would get blacks to come to Norman from Oklahoma City and riot. The majority of people in the neighborhood where we moved were curious about what, not who, was coming. A few people moved out shortly after we moved in, but most of our neighbors decided to outlast us, even the man who believed that God was punishing him by moving the Hendersons into the neighborhood. Garbage was thrown on our lawn, a couple of car windows were broken, and we received obscene phone calls. The words to the Negro spiritual "Nobody Knows the Trouble I've Seen" had special meaning to me and Barbara. Some nights we would look at each other and ask, "When should we leave?" But we decided that we would leave when we got ready, not when other people told us to. During the darkest, most hostile period we met some of our closest, most cherished friends. They gave us moral support and involved us in community and social activities. Our white friends reached across an enormous racial divide to take our hands.

In December 1969, a group of militant black O.U. students summoned me and other black faculty members to a closed meeting, the purpose of which was to belittle those of us committed to nonviolence. My inquisitor was a big, stern-looking student named Calvin. It was rumored that Calvin had once beat up three U.S. marines. When he pointed his long fingers at me and grimaced, I gave him my full attention. "Doc–tor Hen–der–son," he mocked, "We don't need Uncle Toms like you on this campus." The other students were hushed by Calvin's voice. I was hushed by his icy stare. An eerie silence settled in the room as Calvin moved slowly toward the back row where I was sitting. His body began to shake as he moved to within a few steps of me. "You educated, token, proper-talking Negroes are afraid to fight for freedom," he taunted me. A couple of students yelled, "Right on, brother, tell it like it is." I stood up slowly, trying to control a nervous twitch. Then I looked past Calvin to the students sitting near me. "It's true," I said to them. "I don't believe in using violence, but I do believe in finding other ways to obtain racial equality. Obviously, I'm not needed in your civil rights organization. So I won't stay here to be verbally abused." As I walked out of the room, I was aware that I was sweating. I felt fear, sadness, and anger. I was afraid my relationship with the students had ended. I was sad because the students in the room would not accept those of us who did not agree to advocate the use of violence as a civil rights tactic. And I was angry that the students thought I didn't care about them. I went home.

Three hours later, I was awakened from a sound sleep by a ringing telephone. "Dr. Henderson," the voice at the other end of the line began. "This is Judge Brown. A student name Calvin has been arrested, and he has given your name as a reference. If you vouch for him, Dr. Henderson, I'll release him on his own recognizance." Without hesitation I said, "I'll vouch for him, Judge Brown. May I speak with Calvin?" "Hi, Doc," a small voice at the other end of the line whispered. "Merry Christmas, Calvin," I said. "I've just given you the gift of freedom. If there is anything else this Uncle Tom can do for you, let me know." He and I laughed as I put down the telephone receiver. I then realized that the struggle to help black students would not be solely a black versus white confrontation. There would be conflicts among blacks too.

Also in 1969, I was granted tenure, promoted to full professor of education, and appointed Sylvan N. Goldman professor of human relations and given the task of designing a master's degree curriculum in human relations. Thus

I became the first black distinguished professor at the University of Oklahoma. Life was not going to become less stressful for me. But I had survived the middle passage of my career.

References

Acuna, Armando. (1989). "Home Savings Named in Redlining Suit." *Los Angeles Times*, January 1, metro section, 3, San Diego County edition.

Aldridge, Delores. (1991). *Focusing: Black Male-Female Relationships*. Dubuque, IA: Kendall-Hunt.

Anderson, Monica F. (1994). *Black English Vernacular: From "Ain't" to "Yo Mama": The Words Politically Correct Americans Should Know*. Highland City, FL: Rainbow Books.

Baldwin, James. (1961). *Nobody Knows My Name*. New York: Dial Press.

———. (1964). *The Fire Next Time*. New York: Dell.

Bambara, Toni Cade. (1974). *Sea Birds Are Still Alive*. New York: Dial Press.

Billingsley, Andrew. (1992). *Climbing Jacob's Ladder: The Enduring Legacy of African-American Families*. New York: Simon & Schuster.

Billingsley, Andrew, and Cleopatra Howard Caldwell. (1991). "The Church and Family and the School in the African-American Community." *Journal of Negro Education* 60, no. 3 (Summer): 427–40.

Blasco Ibáñez, Vicente. (1919). *The Four Horsemen of the Apocalypse*. Translated by Charlotte B. Johnson. New York: E. P. Dutton.

Boyd, Malcolm. (1971). *Human Like Me, Jesus*. New York: Simon & Schuster.

Brenner, Joel, and Liz Spayd. (1993). "Separate and Unequal: Racial Discrimination in Area Home Lending." *Washington Post*, June 8, A1.

Brimmer, Andrew. (1993). "The Economic Cost of Discrimination." *Black Enterprise* 23, 27.

Brodie, James M. (1993). *Created Equal: The Lives and
Ideals of Black American Innovators*. New York:
William Morrow.

Brooks, Gwendolyn. (1972). *Report from Part One*. Detroit: Broadside.

Carnegie Foundation. (1988). *An Imperiled Generation:
Saving Urban Schools*. Princeton, NJ: Carnegie
Foundation.

Carothers, John C. (1970). *African Mind in Health and
Diseases: A Study of Ethnopsychiatry*. Westport,
CT: Greenwood.

Chambers, James A. (1995). *Blacks and Crime: A Function of Class*. Westport, CT: Praeger.

Clark, Reginald M. (1984). *Family Life and School
Achievement: Why Poor Black Children Succeed
or Fail*. Berkeley: University of California Press.

Clark, William A. V. (1992). "Residential Preferences and
Residential Choices in a Multiethnic Context."
Demography 29, no. 3 (August): 451–66.

Collins, Marva N. (1986). "The Most Unforgettable Person in My Family." *Ebony*, August, 105.

Costen, Melva W. (1993). *African American Christian
Worship*. Nashville, TN: Abingdon.

Dedman, Bill. (1988). "The Color of Money." *Atlanta
Journal and Constitution*, May 15, 19.

Dillard, J. L., ed. (1975). *Perspectives on Black English*.
Hawthorne, NY: Mouton de Gruyter.

Du Bois, W. E. B. (1965). "The Souls of Black Folk." In
Three Negro Classics. New York: Avon Books.
Originally published by A. C. McClung, Chicago,
1903.

Edelman, Marian Wright. (1988). "We Must Convey to the Children That We Love Them." *Ebony*, August, 128–31.

Epstein, Gene. (1996). "Mortgage Against Minorities: Complex Problem, Few Solutions." *Barron's* (January 15): 50.

Evans, Jerry. (1993). *The Afro-American*. San Jose, CA: Magnum Press.

Fairchild, Harold H. (1985). "Black, Negro, or Afro-American? The Differences Are Crucial." *Journal of Black Studies* 16, no. 1 (September): 47–55.

Fanon, Frantz. (1967). *Black Skin, White Masks*. New York: Grove Press.

Farley, Reynolds, Suzanne Bianchi, and Diane Colasanto. (1979). "Barriers to Racial Integration of Neighborhoods." *Annals of the American Academy of Political and Social Science* 441, 97–133.

Federal Reserve Bulletin. (1992). "Expanded HMDA Data on Residential Lending: One Year Later," 78, 11.

Franklin, John Hope. (1988). *From Slavery to Freedom: A History of Negro Americans*. New York: Alfred A. Knopf.

Franklin, John Hope, and Eleanor Holmes Norton, eds. (1989). *Black Initiative and Government Responsibility: An Essay by the Committee on Policy for Racial Justice*. Washington, DC: Joint Center for Political and Economic Studies.

Frazier, E. Franklin. (1957). *Black Bourgeoisie*. New York: Crowell, Collier & Macmillan.

Free, Marvin D. Jr. (1993). *African Americans and the Criminal Justice System*. New York: Garland.

Galen, Michele, and Ann T. Palmer. (1994). "White, Male, and Worried." *Business Week*, January 31, 50-55.

Gist, Noel L., and L. A. Halbert. (1956). *Urban Society*. New York: Thomas Y. Crowell.

Gold, Deborah T. (1990). "Late-Life Sibling Relationships: Does Race Affect Typology Distribution?" *Gerontologists* 30, 741–48.

Gouldner, Helen, with Mary Symons Strong. (1978). *Teachers' Pets, Troublemakers, Nobodies: Black Children in Elementary School.* Westport, CT: Greenwood Press.

Hale, Janice C. (1982). *Black Children: Their Roots, Culture, and Learning Styles.* Provo, UT: Brigham Young University Press.

Hall, Edward T. (1976). *Beyond Culture.* New York: Doubleday.

Hare, Nathan, and Julia Hare. (1984). *The Endangered Black Family: Black Male-Female Relationships.* San Francisco: Black TT.

Harris, Louis, and Associates. (1993). *The Harris Survey Yearbook of Public Opinions.* New York: Louis Harris and Associates.

Haskins, James. (1977). *Barbara Jordan.* New York: Dial Press.

Haynes, Norris M. (1993). *Critical Issues in Educating African-American Children.* New York: IAAS.

Hecht, Michael C., Mary J. Collier, and Sidney A. Ribeau. (1993). *African American Communication: Ethnic Identity and Cultural Interpretation.* Newbury Park, CA: Sage.

Henderson, George. (1989). *A Practitioner's Guide to Understanding Indigenous and Foreign Cultures.* Springfield, IL: Charles C. Thomas.

Hill, Robert B. (1971). *The Strengths of Black Families.* New York: Emerson Hall.

———. (1977). *Informal Adoption among Black Families.* Washington, DC: National Urban League.

Hill, Robert B., Andrew Billingsley, Eleanor Ingram, Michelen R. Malson, Roger H. Rubin, Carol B. Stack, James B. Stewart, and James E. Teele. (1989). *Research on African-American Families: A Holis-*

tic Perspective. Boston: William Monroe Trotter Institute, University of Massachusetts.

Hughes, Langston. (1966). *Book of Negro Humor.* New York: Knopf.

Hurston, Zora Neale. (1942). *Dust Tracks on a Road.* New York: J. B. Lippincott.

Irvine, Jacqueline J. (1991). *Black Students and School Failure: Policies, Practices, and Prescriptions.* Westport, CT: Greenwood Press.

Jackman, Mary R., and Robert W. Jackman. (1980). "Racial Inequalities in Home Ownership." *Social Forces 58,* no. 4 (June): 1221–1234.

Jones, Gayl. (1975). *Corregidora.* Boston: Beacon Press.

Jones, Jacqueline. (1993). *The Dispossessed: America's Underclass from the Civil War to the Present.* New York: Basic Books.

King, Martin Luther Jr. (1963). *Why We Can't Wait.* New York: The American Library.

Kirschenman, Jolene, and Kathryn M. Neckerman. (1991). "'We'd Love to Hire Them, but...': The Meaning of Race for Employers." In *The Urban Underclass,* edited by Christopher Jencks and Paul E. Patterson, 202-32. Washington, DC: Brookings Institution.

Kluckhohn, Florence R., and Fred L. Strodtbeck. (1961). *Variations in Value Orientations.* Evanston, IL: Row, Peterson.

Kochman, Thomas. (1981). *Black and White Styles in Conflict.* Chicago: University of Chicago Press.

Konvitz, Milton R. (1961). *A Century of Civil Rights.* New York: Columbia University Press.

La Rochefoucauld, François. (1936). *The Maxims.* Translated by Louis Kronenberger. New York: Stackpole Sons.

Ladson-Billings, Gloria. (1994). *The Dreamkeepers: Successful Teachers of African American Children.* San Francisco: Jossey-Bass.

Lake, Robert. (1981). *The New Suburbanites: Race and Housing in the Suburbs.* New Brunswick, NJ: Center for Urban Policy Research.

Lanza, Michael L. (1990). *Agrarianism and Reconstruction Politics: The Southern Homestead Act.* Baton Rouge: Louisiana State University Press.

Laye, Camara. (1954). *The Dark Child: The Autobiography of an African Boy.* New York: Farrar, Straus & Giroux.

Lehman, H. Jane. (1991). "Is Secondary Mortgage Market Showing Bias?" *Chicago Tribune,* June 17, 1D.

Lincoln, C. Eric. (1986). "The Black Church and Black Self-Determination." Paper read at a meeting of the Association of Black Foundation Executives, Kansas City, Missouri, April 15.

Los Angeles Times. (1989). "Blacks Rejected More Often Than Whites for Home Loans, Survey Shows." January 23, business section, 2.

Majors, Richard, and Janet M. Billson. (1993). *Cool Pose: The Dilemma of Black Manhood in America.* New York: Lexington Books.

Massey, Douglas S. (1990). "American Apartheid: Segregation and the Making of the Underclass." *American Journal of Sociology* 96, no. 2 (September): 329–57.

McAdoo, Harriette Pipes, ed. (1988). *Black Families.* 2d ed. Beverly Hills, CA: Sage.

McAdoo, Harriette Pipes, and John L. McAdoo, eds. (1985). *Black Children: Social, Educational, and Parental Environments.* Beverly Hills, CA: Sage.

Mukenge, Ida R. (1983). *The Black Church in Urban America: A Case Study in Political Economy.* Lanham, MD: University Press of America.

Myrdal, Gunnar. (1944). *An American Dilemma.* New York: Harper.

Oliver, Melvin L., and Thomas M. Shapiro. (1995). *Black Wealth/White Wealth: A New Perspective on Racial Inequality.* New York: Routledge.

Ploski, Harry A., and James Williams, eds. (1992). *Reference Library of Black Americans.* Four volumes. Detroit: Gale Research.

Powell, John. (1969). *Why Am I Afraid to Tell You Who I Am?* Chicago: Argus Communications.

Puente, Maria. (1996). "War of Words over 'Ebonics'." *USA Today,* December 23, 3A.

Riley, Dorothy Winbush, ed. (1993). *My Soul Looks Back, 'Les I Forget: A Collection of Quotations of People of Color.* New York: HarperCollins.

Rodgers-Rose, LaFrances, ed. (1980). *The Black Woman.* Beverly Hills, CA: Sage.

Rogers, Carl R. (1958). "The Characteristics of a Helping Relationship." *Personnel & Guidance Journal* 37, (September): 6–16.

Seymour, Dorothy Z., ed. (1972). "Black English." *Intellectual Digest* 2, no. 6 (February): 78–80.

Slaughter, Diana T., ed. (1988). *Black Children and Poverty: A Developmental Perspective.* San Francisco: Jossey-Bass.

Solomon, Charlene Marmer. (1992). "Keeping Hate Out of the Workplace." *Personnel Journal* 71, no. 7 (July): 30–36.

Stack, Carol. (1974). *All Our Kin: Strategies for Survival in the Black Community.* New York: Harper & Row.

Sudarkasa, Niera. (1993). "Female-headed African-American Households: Some Neglected Dimensions." In *Family Ethnicity,* edited by Harriette Pipes McAdoo. Newbury Park, CA: Sage.

Tatum, Beverly Daniel. (1992). *Assimilation Blues: Black Families in a White Community.* New York: Hazel-Maxwell.

Taylor, Clyde. (1976). "Soul Talk: A Key to Black Cultural Attitudes." In *Black Awareness: Implications for Black Patient Care,* edited by Dorothy Luckraft. New York: American Journal of Nursing.

Terrell, Henry S. (1971). "Wealth Accumulation of Black and White Families: The Empirical Evidence." *Journal of Finance* 26, (May): 363–77.

Thomas, Donna Neal. (1981). "Black American Health Care." In *Transcultural Health Care,* edited by George Henderson and Martha Primeaux. Menlo Park, CA: Addison-Wesley.

Thomas, R. Roosevelt Jr. (1990). "From Affirmative Action to Affirming Diversity." *Harvard Business Review,* 68, 107–17.

Thompson, Daniel E. (1974). *Sociology of the Black Experience.* Westport, CT: Greenwood Press.

Torrance, E. Paul. (1970). "What It Means to Be Human." In *To Nurture Humanness: Commitment for the 70s,* edited by Mary-Margaret Scobey and Grace Graham. Washington, DC: Association for Supervision and Curriculum Development.

U.S. Bureau of the Census. (1992). *Current Population Reports: Consumer Income.* Series P60, no. 175. Poverty in the United States. Washington, DC: U.S. Government Printing Office.

Walker, Alice. (1983). *In Search of Our Mothers' Gardens.* New York: Harcourt Brace Jovanovich.

Wallace, Michele. (1979). *Black Macho and the Myth of the Black Superwoman.* New York: Dial Press.

Washington, Joseph R. Jr. (1994). *Black Religion: The Negro and Christianity in the United States.* Boston: Beacon Press.

Washington, Robert O. (1982). "Social Development: A Focus for Practice and Education." *Social Work* 27, no. 1 (January): 104–09.

West, Cornel. (1993). *Race Matters.* Boston: Beacon Press.

Whitaker, Catherine J. (1990). *Black Victims.* Washington, DC: U.S. Department of Justice.

White, Joseph L., and Thomas A. Parham. (1990). *The Psychology of Blacks.* Englewood Cliffs, NJ: Prentice-Hall.

Willie, Charles V. (1981). *A New Look at Black Families.* 2d ed. Bayside, NY: General Hall.

Woods, Marilyn J. (1994). *African American Adult Sibling Relationships: A Search for Correlates and Expressions of Affect.* Unpublished dissertation, University of Oklahoma.

Wright, Richard. (1941). *12 Million Black Voices: A Folk History of the Negro in the United States.* New York: Viking.

Young, Whitney M. Jr. (1972). *Beyond Racism.* New York: McGraw-Hill.

Zuckoff, Mitchell. (1992). "Mortgage Gap Still Exists for Minorities." *Boston Globe*, September 27, metro section, 1.

Recommended Readings

Allen, Walter. (1982). *College in Black and White: Black Student Experiences on Black and White Campuses.* Monograph series. Ann Arbor: Center for Afro-American and African Studies, University of Michigan.

Allport, Gordon W. (1954). *The Nature of Prejudice.* New York: Addison-Wesley.

Anderson, Elijah. (1990). *Streetwise: Race, Class, and Change in an Urban Community.* Chicago: University of Chicago Press.

Aoyagi, Kiyotaka. (1988). "The Realm of Personal Attachment in the U.S.A." *International Journal of Sociology of the Family* 18, 215–31.

Asante, Molefi Kete, and William B. Gudykunst, eds. (1989). *Handbook of International and Intercultural Communication.* Newbury Park, CA: Sage.

Banks, James A., and Cherry A. Banks. (1993). *Multicultural Education: Issues and Perspectives.* 2d ed. Boston: Allyn & Bacon.

Bartlett, Donald L., and James B. Steele. (1992). *America: What Went Wrong?* Kansas City, MO: Andrews and McMeel.

Bell, Derrick. (1992). *Faces at the Bottom of the Well.* New York: Basic Books.

Blackwell, James. (1985). *The Black Community: Diversity and Unity.* New York: Dodd, Mead.

223

Comer, James P. (1988). *Maggie's American Dream: The Life and Times of a Black Family.* New York: New American Libary.

Coner-Edwards, Alice, and Jean Spurlock, eds. (1988). *Black Families in Crisis: The Middle Class.* New York: Brunner/Mazel.

Danziger, Sheldon, and Peter Gottschalk, eds. (1993). *Uneven Tides: Rising Inequality in America.* New York: Russell Sage Foundation.

Darity, William A. Jr., and Samuel L. Meyers Jr. (1981). "The Class Character of the Black Middle Class: Polarization between the Black Managerial Elite and the Black Underclass." *Black Law Journal* 7, no. 1: 21–31.

Davis, David B. (1966). *The Problem of Slavery in Western Culture.* Ithaca, NY: Cornell University Press.

Dewart, Janet, ed. (1990). *The State of Black America, 1990.* New York: National Urban League.

Dressler, William W. (1985). "Extended Family Relationships, Social Support, and Mental Health in a Southern Black Community." *Journal of Health & Social Behavior* 26, no. 26 (March): 39–48.

Dunier, Mitchell. (1992). *Slim's Table: Race, Masculinity, and Respectability.* Chicago: University of Chicago Press.

Fainstein, Norman I. (1993). "Race, Class, and Segregation." *International Journal of Urban & Regional Research* 17, 384–403.

Farley, Reynolds, and William H. Frey. (1994). "Changes in the Segregation of Whites from Blacks during the 1980s: Small Steps toward a More Integrated Society." *American Sociological Review* 59, no. 1: 23–45.

Feagin, Joe R., and Melvin P. Sikes. (1994). *Living with Racism: The Black Middle-Class Experience.* Boston: Beacon Press.

Foster, Herbert J. (1983). "African Patterns in the Afro-American Family." *Journal of Black Studies* 14, no. 2 (December): 201–32.

Fraser, George. (1994). *Success Runs in Our Race: The Complete Guide to Effective Networking in the African-American Community.* New York: William Morrow.

Garwood, N. Alfred. (1993). *Black America: A Statistical Sourcebook.* Boulder, CO: Numbers and Concepts.

Greenhouse, Steven. (1993). "Fed Stops Bank Merger, Citing Bias in Lending." *New York Times,* November 17, Section D, 2.

Hacker, Andrew. (1992). *Two Nations: Black and White, Separate, Hostile, Unequal.* New York: Scribner's.

Harrison, Bennett, and Barry Bluestone. (1988). *The Great U-Turn: Corporate Restructuring and the Polarizing of America.* New York: Basic Books.

Henderson, George. (1994). *Cultural Diversity in the Workplace: Issues and Strategies.* Westport, CT: Quorum Books.

———. (1994). *Social Work Interventions: Helping People of Color.* Westport, CT: Bergin & Garvey.

Henderson, George, and Thompson Olasiji. (1995). *Migrants, Immigrants and Slaves: Racial and Ethnic Groups in America.* Lanham, MD: University Press of America.

Hill, Robert B. (1972). *The Strengths of Black Families.* New York: Emerson Hall.

Jackson, James S., ed. (1991). *Life in Black America.* Newbury Park, CA: Sage.

Jackson, Kenneth T. (1985). *Crabgrass Frontier: The Suburbanization of the United States.* New York: Oxford University Press.

Jaynes, Gerald D., and Robin M. Williams, eds. (1990). *A Common Destiny: Blacks and American Society.* Washington, DC: National Academy Press.

Jenkins, Adelbert H. (1982). *The Psychology of the Afro-American: A Humanistic Approach.* New York: Pergamon Press.

Kasarda, John D. (1990). "Structural Factors Affecting the Location and Timing of Underclass Growth." *Urban Geography* 11, no. 3 (May/June): 234–64.

Kozol, Jonathan. (1991). *Savage Inequalities: Children in America's Schools.* New York: Crown.

Landry, Bart. (1988). *The New Black Middle Class.* Berkeley: University of California Press.

Lehman, H. Jane. (1991). "Is Secondary Mortgage Showing Bias?" *Chicago Tribune,* March 17, L2.

Quadagno, Jill. (1994). *The Color of Welfare.* New York: Oxford University Press.

Roberts, James D. (1980). *Roots of a Black Future: Family and Church.* Philadelphia: Westminister Press.

Robinson, Lori S. (1993). "Economist: Inequities of the Past Black Progress." *Emerge,* October, 18–20.

Rutledge, Essie Manuel. (1988). "African-American Socialization Experiences by Family Structure." *Journal of Black Studies* 19, no. 2 (December): 204–15.

Smith, Shanna L. (1992). "Looking Honestly at Fair Housing Compliance." Part I. *ABA Bank Compliance,* Autumn: 32–36.

Staples, Robert. (1973). *The Black Woman in America.* Chicago: Nelson-Hall.

Wallace, Charles S. (1985). *The Church in the Life of the Black Family.* Valley Forge, PA: Judson Press.

Washington, Joseph A. (1988). *Black-Race Family Binds and the White-Ethnic Kinship Ties: Reflections on Religion, Race, and Ethnicity in the Reagan Era.* Tampa: Department of Religious Studies, University of South Florida.

Wilson, William J. (1987). *The Truly Disadvantaged: The Inner City, the Underclass, and Public Policy.* Chicago: University of Chicago Press.

Yetman, Norman R., ed. (1991). *Majority and Minority: The Dynamics of Race and Ethnicity in American Life.* 5th ed. Boston: Allyn & Bacon.

Zarembka, Arlene. (1990). *The Urban Housing Crisis.* Westport, CT: Greenwood Press.

Zollar, Ann Creighton, and Julie Honnold. (1988). "Socioeconomic Characteristics and Kin Interaction in Black Middletown." *Western Journal of Black Studies* 12, no. 1 (Spring): 9–18.

Index

P

Reporting of facts, 70
Residential segregation, 99–103, 104
Reverse discrimination, 145, 167, 195
Revivals, 23
Reward, in the workplace, 161
"Rights of the British Colonies," 40
Rillieux, Norbert, 35
Ritualization, 138
Robeson, Paul, 37
Robinson, Jackie, 39
Rogers, Carl R., 68
Role models, 134, 145, 180
Roosevelt, Eleanor, 36
Rules, fairness of in school, 137
Rush, Benjamin, 40

S
Sable, Jean Point du, 35
"Saint Louis Blues" 36
Salem, Peter, 35
Salvation, 22
Schools
    attendance zones for, 106
    racial identity of, 106
    segregation in, 105–06
Segregation, 191
    in the workplace, 155
    laws, 3
    ongoing, 188
Self-acceptance, 33
Self-actualization, 63
Shadow people, 81, 197
Shakespeare, 31
Shapiro, Thomas M., 96
"Short Symphony" 36
Sifford, Charlie, 39
Silence, 53–54
    ongoing problem of, 191

Vocal cues, 49
Voodoo, 24–25
Voters, manipulation of, 113–14

W

Walker, Alice, 84
Walker, David, 39, 41
Waller, Thomas ("Fats"), 37
Wanting to know, 75
Washington, Booker T., 37
Washington, Denzel, 37
Washington, George, 40
Washington, Kenny, 39
Watts, J. C., 178
"We Wear the Mask," 20
Webster, Noah, 40
Weld, Theodore, 41
Wheatley, Phillis, 35
Whitman, Walt, 41
Whittier, John Greenleaf, 41
Why Am I Afraid to Tell You Who I Am?, 70
Wilkins, Roy, 39
Williams, Daniel Hale, 36
Williams, George, 38
Williams, Samuel Ringold, 38
Willis, Bill, 39
Witchcraft, as medicine, 24
Women. *See also* Family, mother-orientation of
    competition for men among, 84–85
    media devaluation of, 33–34
    role of in middle class, 84
Woods, Tiger, 39
Woodson, Carter G., 38
Woolman, John, 40
Work. *See* Affirmative action; Employees; Employment;
    Job identification; Underemployment, causes of;
    Unemployment, causes of
Wright, Richard, 38